TeenSpeak!

A Bewildered Parent's Guide to Teenagers

Linda Meyer

Peterson's
Princeton, New Jersey

Grateful acknowledgment is made to the following for permission to use, adapt, or reprint material: the American Academy of Pediatrics; the American Academy of Child and Adolescent Psychiatry; the University of Michigan's Institute for Social Research Monitoring the Future Program; the Alan Guttmacher Institute; the George H. Gallup International Institute; Yankelovich Partners; Roper Starch Worldwide; the Rand Youth Poll; BKG Youth/New York; Teenage Research Unlimited/Northbrook, Illinois; the Zandl Group/New York; *Seventeen* magazine; the NOW Legal Defense and Education Fund; the Joyce Foundation; Bob DeMoss of Focus on the Family; the Parents Music Resource Center; Zero Population Growth; and the numerous other organizations, individuals, and state and federal government agencies—in particular the U.S. Centers for Disease Control and the National Center for Health Statistics—that provided facts and figures for inclusion in this book.

Library of Congress Cataloging-in-Publication Data

Meyer, Linda, 1950-
Teenspeak : a bewildered parent's guide to teenagers / Linda Meyer.
p. cm.
ISBN 1-56079-338-4
1. Teenagers—United States. 2. Youth—United States—Social conditions. I. Title.
HQ796.M437 1994
305.23'5—dc20 94-21338
CIP

Cover and interior design by Greg Wozney Design, Inc.
Printed in the United States of America
10 9 8 7 6 5 4 3 2 1

This book is dedicated to my parents,
Charles and Betty Meyer, who raised two teenagers—and survived.
And to my daughter, Dana Anne Russ, who will be a teenager all too soon.

TABLE OF CONTENTS

ACKNOWLEDGMENTS

So many people contributed to this book, it would be impossible to thank each one individually. There are some, however, who deserve special mention.

First, to the hundreds of teens from all over the country who shared their hopes, fears, dreams, and a great many other details of their lives, this book would not have been possible without your help and enthusiasm.

To the teenagers of the City Kids Coalition in New York City, who on so many Friday afternoons for the past year allowed me to be a part of their "safe space," thank you for sharing so much of your lives and positive energy. To Mitch Pertiz, co-director of City Kids Coalition, your assistance and your insights have been invaluable. Thanks, also, to City Kids Foundation founder Laurie Meadoff and staffers Alex Atkinson and Carla Harman in New York, and Sheila Nichols, formerly with City Kids in Los Angeles.

To the many dozens of experts who have devoted their lives to the very important work of caring for teenagers and who were consulted in this effort—physicians, psychologists, school administrators, teachers, social workers, youth organization directors, and others—I hope all the wisdom you so generously shared with me has been reflected here. Thanks, too, to the many parents of teens whose experiences provided important information and inspiration.

Special appreciation goes also to Michael Thacker, principal, University City High School, St. Louis; Carol Kolar, English teacher, Parkway North High School, St. Louis; Charlotte Huggins, teacher/newspaper sponsor, New Trier High School, Winnetka, Illinois; Julie Meador, teacher, the Satellite Academy, New York City Public Schools; and Geri Seiner, English/journalism teacher, Taft High School, Los Angeles.

A huge debt of gratitude goes to Marian Salzman of BKG Youth teen marketing research in New York for advice, inspiration and information that were critical along the way. To Chuck Fallis at the Centers for Disease Control, thanks for always being there—and with all the information I needed too. To Joyce Buchanan at the University of Michigan's Institute for Social Research and to Bob Bezilla at the Gallup Organization, thanks for your patience and help. And to the many editors and writers at major magazines addressing teen interests and issues, as well as authors of other books on teens, your time and insights were greatly appreciated. My thanks, too, to Martine Hackett, Sandra Aiken, and Hilary Drummond for their special assistance.

To many friends and relatives, all of whom couldn't possibly be listed here, your support was critical. For their unique and important contributions, my thanks also to Peggy Campbell and Curt

Rowell, Susan and Jack Dulaney, Betti and Paul DuBro, Ava Ehrlich and Barry Freedman, Patricia and Tom Howard, Bonnie Rothman Morris, Esther Lyss, Sarah Metry, Pat and Andrew Fernandez, Amy and Howard Simon, Barbara Unell, Siri Naraine, and Marla Jhingoor; also Ilene Z. Cohen, Ph.D., New York City, who helped me in so many ways. To my attorney, Steven Beer, thank you for your guidance.

To my immediate family, many thanks for your infinite patience. To my husband (and sometimes editor), Len Russ, and to our daughter, Dana, my love and appreciation for giving me the space and support to write this book.

To Kitty Colton, manuscript editor at Peterson's, thanks for your perceptiveness—and patience!—and for making so much so easy. And last but not least, to my editor, Carol Hupping, at Peterson's, thank you for your invaluable guidance, unflagging enthusiasm, unfailing good humor, and, most important, willingness to let the content go where the information took us. This one's for you.

Today's children are tyrants. They disobey their parents, gobble their food, and tyrannize their teachers.

—Socrates, circa 400 B.C.

INTRODUCTION

There are all kinds of teenagers. City slickers and suburban cowboys. Small-town innocents and inner-city sophisticates. Quick wits and nitwits. Scholarship winners and felonious sinners. Sports freaks. Band geeks. Rich, poor, and in-between. Teens on the road to college. Teens on the road to nowhere. They are all our future. And that makes understanding them and the world in which they are coming of age critical to us all.

Parents of teens have never had it easy. Nor have teens themselves. The necessary transition from dependence on the family to independent adulthood, so often discussed by psychologists specializing in the adolescent years, is tough on everybody. But the vast majority of teenagers and their parents get through it just fine. According to Dr. Victor Strasburger, chief of adolescent medicine at the University of New Mexico in Albuquerque, 80 percent of young people make it through their teenage years without any major problems. What's daunting is the notion that 20 percent *don't.*

Today's teenagers need their parents. They need a lot of adults in their lives who care about them and let them know it—day in and day out. This message resonates from conversations with educators, psychologists, physicians, and—the most important experts of all—teenagers themselves.

This book is not intended to be a weighty look at the psychology of the teenage years—many important books for parents have already been written on this subject (and a list of some of them is provided herein). Rather, it aims to freeze this moment in time, to capture some of the major features of the current teenage landscape and look at what they mean and why they may have evolved. Body piercing. Video games. Drugs. Sex. Pregnancy. Gangs. Guns. AIDS. It is all the stuff of which being a teenager is now made. And it matters not who their families are or where they live. There are no "bubbles" for kids to grow up in anymore, though I grew up in one in the late 1960s and perhaps you did too.

How is the world today's teens are growing up in different from the one we, today's *parents*, grew up in? What's going on under all those dreadlocks and ponytails, anyway? What's a wannabe? A blunt? A herb? Who's Doc Marten? Who's Dr. Dre? Why can't kids wear red bandannas to school anymore? And what's a worried parent to do? These are among the major questions this book endeavors to answer for bewildered parents in these times so bewildering for us all.

Who Are These Guys?

Teens in the United States today number around 25 million—from slackers and hackers, to hard workers and homework shirkers, to technoravers and cyberpunks.* Parents, of course, know today's teens best as the once-delightful, once-adoring ten-year-olds who won't talk to them anymore.

The teenagers of today were born between 1975 and 1981 to parents who most likely call themselves part of the baby boom generation. Teens today find themselves with several generational nicknames—having arrived, it seems, just in time to be at the tail end of everything. They are part of the final phase of the "baby busters," the waning years of novelist Douglas Coupland's "Generation X," and the last gasp (or "Nintendo Wave") of the "13th Gen," defined by authors William

---

*Translation for parents: Techno is the dance music of the 1990s, raving is the all-night dance scene that goes with it, and cyberpunks are teen travelers on the information superhighway.

What Do You Call Teenagers?

Whatever you do, don't call them "kids," say pollsters and other pulse-takers of America's 13- to 19-year-olds. "Young adults"—yes. "Young people"—fine. "Students"—that'll do. "Teens," "teenagers"—perfectly okay. Teens, however, say "kids" is all right. It's a term they often use themselves. Still, an effort has been made here to keep use of the word "kids" to a minimum.

Strauss and Neil Howe in their book of that name. For a great many reasons, they are unlike teens from any previous era.

CULTURAL DIVERSITY

Young people today inhabit a world far more culturally diverse than the one their parents grew up in. While their elders were born into a country that was 90 percent white, today's teens make their way in a nation that will gradually shift to 70 percent white in their lifetime. Theirs is an America populated "not only with more blacks and American-born Hispanics but also with the new immigrants of the 1980s and 1990s: Mexicans, Filipinos, Koreans, Cubans, Vietnamese, Indians, Pakistanis, and others from Asia, Africa, and Ireland," notes Les Krantz in *America by the Numbers* (Houghton Mifflin, 1993).

You can see this diversity in the classroom, in the curriculum changes today's students desire. According to a recent Gallup Youth Survey, students across the board want more lessons on the achievements of nonwhite men and, especially, nonwhite women, including Muslims, Asians, and Hispanics.

You can see this diversity in young people's relationships as well. Interracial dating occurs far more often than in their parents' day. When surveyed in 1991 for *Seventeen* magazine's Love and Sex in the 1990s survey, conducted by Market Facts, Inc., nearly 40 percent of teenage boys and 35 percent of teenage girls said they had dated someone of another race. Half of the boys and 44 percent of the girls said they "probably would" or "definitely would" date someone of another race.

"Black influence has become a major force in leading teen lifestyles," according to veteran teen market researcher Peter Zollo, president of Teenage Research Unlimited in Northbrook, Illinois. "Rap, dance, and R&B have dominated radio and video airplay for teens. And even on the most mainstream media—network TV—shows that feature black actors . . . have become teen favorites. African-American influence extends into teen language, fashion, and beauty choices."

DIVORCE AND SINGLE-PARENT HOMES

Young people today are the product of one of the most significant changes in the history of the American family: the increase in single-parent families. The parents of one million children divorce each year, according to U.S. Census figures. Whereas 10 percent of children under 18 were living in one-parent families in 1960, 25 percent live in one-parent families now, the Census Bureau finds. According to figures from a 1994 report by the Carnegie Corporation of New York, the parents of almost 50

What Do You Call Dark-Skinned People?

Even dark-skinned people don't agree on this one. According to a report in *American Demographics* magazine, a 1993 Roper Poll found that 42 percent of non-Hispanic dark-skinned adults preferred to be called "black," while 30 percent preferred "African American." Younger dark-skinned people preferred "African American" to "black" by a slight margin. "Black," however, remains the term of choice at the U.S. Census Bureau. All this considered, "black" is the term you'll find in this book.

"I have a friend whose parents got divorced, and neither one wanted the children," says Laura,* a Tampa teen, with a note of sadness in her voice. "It was really hard for her at first. But she's doing better with it."

***Names followed by an asterisk have been changed at the participants' request.**

percent of children under age 18 now get divorced, and those children spend at least several years in a single-parent household.

"Divorce and its attendant confusion and impoverishment" have become "the central fear" of this generation of young people, write William Strauss and Neil Howe in *Generations* (William Morrow, 1991). "Coping with the debris, America's 1970s-era children [among them, youth who are teenagers today] went from a family culture of *My Three Sons* to one of *My Two Dads.* " Research on how family members feel following a split shows "four-fifths of today's divorced adults profess to being happier afterward, but a majority of their children feel otherwise," the authors report.

A San Diego pediatrician relates, "The parent of a 17-year-old called me the other day, worried because her son had asked her, 'How come you and Dad aren't divorced? Everyone else's parents are.' " Teenagers of parents who *do* stay together feel anxious, vulnerable, and especially fearful any time their parents argue, says Barbara Ilardi, Ph.D., professor of psychology at the University of Rochester in Rochester, New York.

HOME ALONE

Today's teenagers are far more likely to have grown up with mothers who work. It has been estimated that more than three-quarters of American teens today come home to an empty house after school. Home alone, many also shoulder household responsibilities like doing the grocery shopping and laundry and making dinner. Three-quarters of women with children ages 6 to 17 now have jobs. In 1990, the U.S. Bureau of Labor Statistics found that 60 percent of women with children under age 6 were working outside the home, compared with 20 percent in 1960.

"While their environment has become more threatening, teenagers have become less connected with their families. Just 63 percent of families with children eat dinner together frequently," note the authors of *The Adolescent and Young Adult Fact Book,* published by the Children's Defense Fund in 1991. Almost one in five sixth- through twelfth-graders surveyed reported "they had not had a ten-minute conversation with one of their parents within the previous month."

ALL WORK AND NO PLAY

Another common feature of teenage life in the 1990s is a part-time or full-time job. Many teens work 20 hours a week or more. Time for other types of extracurricular activity is increasingly limited. Regular vigorous physical activity among teens, for instance, has dropped by almost half since 1984, according to the U.S. Centers for Disease Control.

WHAT AGE DO TEENS *WANT* TO BE?

Teenage Research Unlimited in Northbrook, Illinois, asked teens that question a couple of years ago, and Chris Efken, a veteran youth marketing researcher with the organization, reports on their findings: "Twelve-year-olds said 17. The reason is that they look at 17-year-olds and see they can drive, they have later curfews, they seem to have it all. Then when you talk to 17- and 18-year-olds, they want to be two or three years older—either in college and away from parents or working full time, where there are no administrative rules like in school. When you start talking to

the twentysomethings, they want to be three years younger."
In a 1994 survey by the Zandl Group, a New York City marketing consulting firm specializing in the youth market, teenage boys said they wanted to be 21 so they could drink legally or 18 so they could move out of the house; they also said they would like to be 4, since that would be a lot easier. Teenage girls also said they'd like to be 21 to drink legally and 16 so they could drive; they also wanted to be 5 so they could be carefree.

"It's a myth that teens lead carefree lives with little responsibility," says Marian Salzman, head of BKG Youth, a New York–based marketing research firm that focuses on young people's tastes and attitudes. Combine a job with household duties, school-related extracurricular and academic responsibilities, and volunteer work (a must for today's college-bound), says Salzman, "and you'll realize that many teens put in far more than a 40-hour workweek."

WHEN DO KIDS GET TO BE KIDS?

A major theme that echoes through interviews with teenagers and professionals who work with them is the early loss of childhood many young people experience today. Too many teens, they say, have taken on the role of the parent. Too many parents are overwhelmed by personal problems and have slipped into the role of the child.

The scene is the basement gathering room of the City Kids Foundation in New York City one recent Friday night. Fifty or so multicultural teenagers gather for their weekly coalition meeting to hear a talk by the dynamic Verna Eggleston, a former New York City deputy administrator for child welfare who has more charisma than any fire-and-brimstone preacher. Reading from that week's newspaper headlines, she outlines the major features of her audience's daily life: teens shooting each other in the streets, decaying schools, disintegrating families. As she finishes, anger rises in her voice. "When do *you* get to be teenagers?" she booms. "When do *you* get to be kids?" A murmur of agreement goes up from the teens. Tears well up in most eyes. She has struck a terrible and too familiar chord.

SCHOOL AS PARENT

"I don't think we have enough adults for all the kids we've got," says Loeb Aronin, Ed.D., director of psychological services for the Los Angeles Unified Public Schools, who has worked in education for 38 years and supervises a district staff of nearly 400 psychologists.

"There are so many things happening that are so much more difficult for kids now. They're carrying a lot of weight in terms of what's going on in their own families—divorce, problems brothers and sisters have, transience," Aronin says. One nationwide trend he sees is schools serving as the providers and coordinators of a wide range of social services. "Families are so needy," he explains. "Someone needs to be a case manager for the family. Kids today need lots of people in their lives who will say to them, 'I do care about you. You're important. I'm going to make sure you're protected.' "

"It's not enough to be good at sports now. Kids have to shoot for the Olympics."

—Soccer and hockey team member Ryan Dulaney, 14, Parkway North High School, Chesterfield, Missouri

Sadly, many more young people would like to attend college than can afford to. According to the 1993 Nickelodeon/Yankelovich Youth Monitor U.S., 89 percent of 14- to 15-year-olds say they want to go to college; only 52 percent of them believe they will be able to afford to go.

STRESSED FOR SUCCESS

In the suburbs and in the cities, another kind of stress plays a role in the lives of many teens—the stress caused by parents who care *too much* about what their children achieve.

"Nice job on the science project, Mrs. Green," calls out 15-year-old Jeff*, a high school student in an upscale Midwestern suburb, as his buddy's mother picks up her son from school. Jeff explains, "A lot of parents do their kids' homework. They think it helps them to get ahead." But Jeff says he's worried about his friend. "His parents do everything for him. I don't know what he's going to do when he gets to college and is on his own."

According to Danielle* of New Trier High School in suburban Chicago, "Parents also let their kids out of going to class if they're not ready for a test or let them stay home to work on a paper. I really think that's wrong. It's not fair to the kids who do all their work and *don't* stay home to finish things." She continues, "The parents will write a note that says the student didn't feel well. They'll even lie. I guess a lot of people think this is okay because it's part of getting ahead. But I don't agree. I think if you're not prepared, then you just have to take the test anyway and not do well on it."

BAD NEWS BEARS

Teens in the 1990s are operating under a blanket of negative news about themselves, their futures, and the biggest institution in their lives besides their families: their schools. They hear constantly about the "dumbing down" of American education—*their* education. Evening newscasts and front-page headlines tell them time and again that their schools are in crisis or just no good.

Today's teens don't want to learn—or, worse, can't learn—or so they are told. Their test scores trend down, they hear. (Actually, SAT scores rose slightly in 1993—a story relegated to the fine print.) Recently, the SAT was revamped to include the use of calculators for the math section, which many viewed as a concession to a current crop of less competent students (though others say this is not the case). Also recently, the Educational Testing Service took the "aptitude" out of the Scholastic Aptitude Test, renaming it the Scholastic Assessment Test.

Honors programs and "tracking" for brighter students have been eliminated at many schools on the theory that poorer students suffer when such distinctions are made. ("But what about the better students?" wonder the better students and their parents, as they make the shift to private schools if they can afford it.)

God Is "In" Among Teens

Just when you thought this generation of teens might be hopelessly lost comes word from a 1993 Gallup Youth Survey that teens are actually *more* likely than adults to be found in church. Nearly half of teens surveyed said in a typical week they attend religious services at least once. Among adults, 40 percent attend church weekly. Regular church-going, the poll found, was more common among teens ages 13 to 15 (54 percent) than among those 16 and older (44 percent). Sixty-eight percent of black teens reported attending church in the previous week, compared with 48 percent of white teens.

Issues Teens Care About Most in 1994

1. AIDS
2. Education
3. Race relations
4. Violence
5. Abortion
6. Child abuse
7. The environment
8. Drinking and driving
9. Drug abuse
10. The economy

Source: Teenage Research Unlimited, Northbrook, Illinois

SCHOOL DAZE

School programs that teenagers in the 1960s and 70s took for granted, such as athletics, music, and art, have been the budget cutback casualties of recent years in school districts from coast to coast.

At many schools, too many students don't even bother to show up. Getting young people to school on time—or at all—is a major headache for principals across the country. Keeping them out of the halls and in class is a problem of unprecedented proportions, educators say. This year, communities from Florida to California, from Ohio to Texas, began using laws long at their disposal to hold parents legally responsible when their children are truant.

"Apathy on the part of students is probably the number one problem in education today," says Michael Thacker, principal at University City High School in St. Louis. "In the late 1960s and into the 1970s, when there was a lot of adolescent revolt going on and kids were questioning everything, we didn't question our teachers," adds Thacker, a teenager himself during those years. "We just did our assignments. There was peer pressure to do what the teacher said and a clear message from home and society that if you do this you will succeed. That doesn't exist today. Today the peer pressure says, 'Let's get by with what we can get by with.' There is no frightening home consequence."

Whereas today's generation of parents was virtually guaranteed that an education would lead to a job, Thacker continues, "because of today's economic changes, kids no longer have that. In terms of teen culture, there seems to be a sense that education is not that important, not a key to opening doors."

THEIR PROSPECTS FOR THE FUTURE

The news about their futures, teens hear, is equally grim. They wonder if the courses they're taking now will be relevant to *anything* down the line and whether the career paths they choose will lead anywhere. (One-third of college grads today hold jobs that don't require a college degree, or so goes a statistic they read time and again.) Also, they hear, they'll be part of the first generation since the Civil War unable to match their parents' standard of living. And they are constantly reminded that they're likely to spend the rest of their lives dealing with the federal deficit.

TEEN VIOLENCE

New and frightening threads weave through the fabric of American teenage life, shaping not only current teenage culture but the adults these young people will become. Their world is far different from the one their parents knew growing up.

Teens Are Often Victims of Violence

Life is not a safe proposition for American teenagers in the 1990s. Nearly 1 in 4 violent crimes in this country in 1992 involved a victim between ages 12 and 17, an increase of 14 percent since 1987. The perpetrators included both other teens and adults.

Almost 1 in 13 juveniles (ages 12 to 17) reported being victims of violent crime in 1992—up from almost 1 in 17 in 1987. For people age 35 and older, the crime rate was about 1 in 81.

Source: U.S. Justice Dept. Office of Juvenile Justice and Delinquency Prevention Report on Juvenile Victimization: 1987-1992, released June 1994

Which Issues Are "In" This Year?

77% say caring about the environment is "in"
75% say eating healthy is "in"
60% say sharing costs on a date is "in" (more girls say this than boys)
58% say volunteering is "in"
49% say being patriotic is "in"
47% say caring about politics is "in"
45% say protesting is "in"
42% say the military is "in"
42% say being politically correct is "in"

Source: Teenage Research Unlimited, Northbrook, Illinois

Homicide, for instance, is touching—and ending—teenage lives in greater numbers than ever before. "Violence is devastating this generation as surely as polio cut down young people 40 years ago," noted *Newsweek* in its 1993 cover story "Teen Violence: Wild in the Streets." U.S. Attorney General Janet Reno has called youth violence "the greatest single crime problem in America today."

More than 2,400 teenagers between the ages of 15 to 19 are killed in firearm homicides each year, according to 1992 FBI figures. That's at least six young people murdered every day. While much of this is urban violence, studies find the presence of guns in today's youth culture crosses all racial, cultural, geographic, and economic lines. Nearly one in four students reports having been the victim of violence on or near school property.

OTHER DEADLY THREATS

Drug abuse—the scourge of teenage life in the 70s—is, while not the problem it once was, again on the increase, particularly among younger teens. Alcohol is the biggest concern; it is, by far, the substance most widely abused by teens. Nearly 30 percent of high school seniors in a major national study reported binge drinking—consuming five or more drinks in a row—in the previous two-week period. Cigarette smoking, while down from the mid-70s, remains popular among teens, with some 25 percent of seniors leaving high school as smokers.

Then there's suicide, now among the leading causes of death for teens. In the course of my research for this book, most of the teens I talked with seemed to know *somebody* who had jumped off a highway overpass, put a gun to his head, or taken a lethal drug overdose.

The specter of AIDS also haunts this generation of teens. But while many students have armed themselves with information, chastity agreements, or condoms, large numbers of teens practice unprotected sex—as the more than one million teenage pregnancies each year attest. As far as sex goes, more teens are having it and at ever-younger ages. Today's teens find they must take a stand on sexual issues—and define themselves sexually—sometimes even before they reach their teens.

THEIR WORLD

Sit around with a bunch of today's teenagers and ask them about critical moments from history as they've lived it and what will you hear? One thing is: "I'm too young to remember when *Reagan* was shot." You heard me—Reagan, *not* Kennedy. And while the generation that gave birth to today's teens thrilled to NASA's achievements in space, their offspring were chilled by the horrifying images of the space shuttle *Challenger* disaster.

The cold war is over. So are the massive demonstrations against the Vietnam War in which so many parents of today's teens took part. The war

Today's Teens Often Get a Bad Rap

Teens today deserve a lot more credit than some people give them, according to Marian Salzman of BKG Youth (a teen marketing research organization). Salzman spends her life traveling the country and taking the pulse of teenage opinion and style. ("I've sat in so many fast-food places and had so much diet soda I'm amazed I have kidneys left," she jokes.) Her findings are taken extremely seriously by clients like Nintendo of America, Levis, Kodak, and MasterCard.

Says Salzman, "It's a myth that teens care only about them-

selves. Teens of all ages have evolved into an eco-generation that values quality, durability . . . and value. Simplicity is big, wholesomeness is back, and concern for common causes is par for the course.

"Teens of this generation know it is up to them to put this country on its feet again," she adds, pointing out that they are active volunteers for causes in their communities and the larger world.

Salzman finds that teens are not materialistic but, rather, hard-working and "turned off by the consumerism of recent years." She says they *do* read—"30 percent of teens surveyed indicated that they read fiction outside of

teens know now is the Persian Gulf War. They watched it, proudly for the most part, on TV.

The struggle for civil rights in which many of their parents participated continues, though today's teens say it takes a more personal form, in everyday encounters with racism and sexism.

This generation doesn't know a world without homeless people on its streets, without deficits, without alarm systems on houses and cars. The stock market crash of October 1987 is part of its collective experience, along with recession, corporate downsizing, and job displacement—with which their parents may well have been forced to cope. The events they've witnessed so far fuel their trepidation.

THE GOOD NEWS

To be sure, there is a lot of bad news about this generation of teens: bad news about what it's up against, bad news about what some of its members are doing to themselves and others. But there *is* good news—and plenty of it—about these guys too. Happily, many experience much of what their parents remember most fondly from their own teenage years. Take the prom, for instance. It's still a very big deal for most of today's teens. Or getting a driver's license. A great many cite this as the most important moment of their teenage years. The vast majority also say they have good relationships with their parents. For the most part, they want to go to college, get married, and have children. They are optimistic. They are competitive. They know they'll have to work hard to get ahead.

WHAT DOES IT ALL MEAN?

Today's teens are coming of age in times more troubled, more stressful, and more fraught with immediate dangers than anything you, their parents, experienced. But for all that, teenagers are still teenagers. And they still have fun. They experience most of the same emotions, conflicts, and triumphs their parents did as teens. Today's teens are exuberant, energized, embarked on a great adventure. They go to parties, on dates, to malls, to the beach. They recycle. They hang out. They worry about being cool. They eat junk food, do homework, fret over their SATs and college choices, participate in sports, cheerlead, pray, get drunk or drugged, ignore homework. They have their style, their language, their music. They volunteer. They write poetry. They peer counsel. They get pimples. They talk and talk and talk on the phone. And they still can't get their hair to do what they want it to. Also very important in the 90s, they have each other. And they have you, their parents, to rebel against. That part hasn't changed.

the books they are assigned at school"—and that religion is often part of their lives. "More and more teens indicated that praying is the only way to establish calm in their lives," she explains, "and Bible study groups are cropping up in youth circles all over the country."

Teen Roundup

Wazzup?

What's in? Who's in? What are the big issues for teens? What do they worry about? From north, south, east, west, and points between come answers providing parents a cultural portrait of today's adolescents.

The following roundup of high school views and attitudes was compiled from questionnaires and personal interviews with members of high school newspaper and yearbook staffs (four or more students from each school in most instances), conducted at the National Scholastic Press Association convention in Washington, D.C., in November 1993 and followed up by phone in 1994. In the cases of Aloha, Oregon, and Oxford, Alabama, student leaders encountered under the auspices of other organizations were similarly queried.

The views that follow do not reflect the opinions of all students at any given school but are, rather, a sampling of opinions from among their ranks.

SPRING VALLEY HIGH SCHOOL
Columbia, South Carolina
Student body type: 2,700 students, mostly college-bound; 50 percent white, 50 percent black.
Favorite music performers: Hootie & the Blowfish, Blind Melon, Garth Brooks, Pearl Jam. "Dr. Dre is really popular with everybody."
Most fab foods: Pretzels and bagels among the girls—"all the girls at Spring Valley are really concerned with their weight." Among the guys, it's hamburgers and pizza.
Fav thing kids here do with free time: Party.
Fav places to hang out: Rush's ("a fast-food place with numerous restaurants all over Columbia and nowhere else"), parties.
Issues heavy on our minds: Homelessness, pregnancy, death ("because we've had many deaths recently"—car accidents, often drunk driving–related). Also, rezoning (a proposed plan might shift some students to another high school).
Can't-live-without clothing for guys and gals: Anything from the Gap. Jeans. Polos. Hiking boots for girls and guys.
The future looks: "Good for most students."
Our heroes: Rush Limbaugh (among white males), Malcolm X (among black students).
Teens at our school worry most about: Looks, dating, weight (girls). Fights and alcohol (guys).
Weirdest things students at our school do: Pierce body parts, dye hair odd colors.

MIAMI SUNSET SENIOR HIGH SCHOOL
Miami, Florida
Student body type: 2,500 students, grades 9 through 12. Ethnic melting pot: majority Hispanic, also African American, white, Asian, and Caribbean.
Favorite music performers: SWV, Janet Jackson, Tag Team, the Lemonheads, Budja Banton, MC Lyte, Snoop Doggy Dogg, Dr. Dre.
Most fab foods: Chinese, Italian.
Fav places to hang out: Restaurants—Bennigan's, Champions (sports bar). Clubs—The Kitchen, Lime Key, Another World, Cameo, Boomerang's, Paragon, Warsaw, 5th Street. Also, cruising on Ocean Drive and attending "ranch parties."
Fav things kids here do with free time: Work, play sports, play basketball at

Sugarwood Park, work out at Porky's Gym or Spinelli's Gym.
Issues heavy on our minds: Weapons on campus, AIDS awareness, a drug-free environment, graffiti.
Teens at our school worry most about: Grades, college, parents, boyfriend/girlfriend relationships, our own future, appearance, being accepted by other kids.
Can't-live-without clothing for guys and gals: Baseball hats, Doc Martens, Timberlands, jeans, clogs, chokers, Walkmans, denim, vests, hoop earrings.
The future looks: " . . . so bright we gotta wear shades" (senior class picture motto, class of '94).
Our generation of teens is: "Expressive. They wish to be heard. They are individualists. Not following the crowd is admired. So is attending school. It's not nerdy to want to make good grades or do well on the SATs."

UKIAH HIGH SCHOOL
Ukiah, California
Student body type: Small town. 1,200 students, grades 9 through 12; 60 percent white, the rest largely Hispanic.
Favorite music groups: Simon & Garfunkel, Soul Asylum, Pearl Jam, Snoop Doggy Dogg, lots of country.
Most fab food: Mitchell's donuts.
Fav places to hang out: Mitchell's Donut Shop, Schat's Bakery for coffee and muffins, anybody's house to drink beer (or not drink beer), local parks.
Fav things kids here do with free time: Smoke pot, see movies, hang out in coffee houses, go someplace to talk where there are no parents.
Issues heavy on our minds: Environment (air and land), drug prevention, gang prevention.
Can't-live-without clothing for guys and gals: Birkenstocks, baggy jeans. For surf/skater crowd: Stussy and Mossimo brands.
The future looks: " . . . like change, a new course for the nation."
Teens at our school worry most about: Divorce, grades, dying, AIDS. ("Mendocino County has a high percentage of AIDS cases.")
Weirdest things students at our school do: Ice blocking on the golf course, sitting on water towers and drinking.

PELLA COMMUNITY HIGH SCHOOL
Pella, Iowa
Student body type: Small town. 500 students; 85 percent white, 15 percent

Asian. Generally religious, college-bound.
Favorite music performers: Reba McEntire, Eric Clapton, Aerosmith, Metallica; also, 70s rock music is *very* popular—the Who, Led Zeppelin, the Eagles, to name a few.
Most fab food: Sliders at George's Pizza.
Fav places to hang out: School—students are very active. Also, the cliffs above the Des Moines River, Red Rock.
Fav thing kids here do with free time: Cruise around the town square. ("On a good night it's bumper-to-bumper.")
Issues heavy on our minds: Teen pregnancy, the environment.
Can't-live-without clothing for guys and gals: Birkenstocks, baggy jeans, men's boxer shorts worn as shorts by girls, huge sweatshirts.
The future looks: " . . . fuzzy. We're left with a huge deficit and responsibilities. We have the potential to do great things, but will we?"
Our heroes: Athletes.
Teens at our school worry most about: Homework, term papers, tests.

WESTERVILLE NORTH HIGH SCHOOL
Westerville, Ohio (outside Columbus)
Student body type: Large, suburban school, upper-middle-class community. 2,000 students, grades 9 through 12; largely white, small percentage of minorities. Competitive.
Favorite music performers: Pearl Jam, Dr. Dre, Cypress Hill, Garth Brooks, Hank Williams Jr.
Most fab food: Loaves of fresh bread from the Harvest Bread Co.
Fav places to hang out: Denny's, movies, drinking spots, local dam, lake, parks, anyplace with no parents.
Fav things kids here do with free time: Get drunk, go to parties, get high, go to movies, bowl, play miniature golf, go cruising, hang out.
Issues heavy on our minds: AIDS, drunk driving, drug abuse, racism.
Our heroes: Sports figures; celebrities; our principal, Mr. McCann.
Teens at our school worry most about: College, racial tension, appearance, death.
Weirdest thing students at our school do: Bleacher diving—teens stand at the top of bleachers and dive into the crowd or into the arms of friends standing below.
Our generation of teens is: "Self-centered, somewhat superficial, but aware of social problems because of music and media—e.g., they want to legalize drugs

because of [the rap group] Cypress Hill. Some teens are working to improve things."

OXFORD HIGH SCHOOL
Oxford, Alabama (40 miles from Birmingham)
Student body type: Very rural. 1,500 students, grades 7 through 12; 70 percent white, 30 percent minority—mostly black. College-bound.
Favorite music performers: Country! Garth Brooks, Reba McEntire, Alabama, Mark Chesnutt, Clint Black, Wynonna Judd. "If it's not country, it's stuff like Janet Jackson or Mariah Carey."
Most fab food: Pineapple pizza. "It's just like it sounds. You can get it at any of the pizza places. We have five."
Fav places to hang out: The mall, Moore's Fun Center ("people go there for go-carts, batting cages, the video arcade, and billiards—they also cruise it on weekends"), Oxford Lake, movies, C.C. ("a clearing on top of Cheaha Mountain where we have bonfires"). Driving to Birmingham to go to teenage clubs is also popular.
Fav things kids here do with free time: Participate in school sports ("our teams are tops in the state, and our cheerleaders are ranked second in the nation"), hang out with friends, go for car rides with friends, take part in family events.
Issues heavy on our minds: Drug awareness, the environment, leadership, fellowship of our fellow students.
Can't-live-without clothing for guys and gals: Levis jeans, big-legged pants (girls). Flannel shirts, jeans, name brands (guys). Cowboy boots are a big thing now.
The future looks: " . . . very promising for students at Oxford High School. We are very disciplined and educated and are able to show good, sportsmanlike conduct."
Our heroes: Parents, fellow students.
Students at our school worry most about: Social problems, grades, sports.

ALOHA HIGH SCHOOL
Aloha, Oregon (suburban Portland)
Student body type: Suburban. 1,300 students, grades 10 through 12; 80 percent white, 20 percent minority—largely Hispanic and Asian. Mostly college-bound.
Favorite music performers: R&B—Boyz II Men; country—Alan Jackson, Garth Brooks; top 40—Mariah Carey, Whitney Houston; rap—Dr. Dre; alternative/thrash—Pearl

Jam, Blind Melon, Stone Temple Pilots, Alice in Chains.

Most fab foods: Hole-ly Fries (flat fries with waffle-iron pattern) with a chocolate milk shake at Red Robin's; also, their "mud pie." Pineapple and Canadian bacon pizza (it's just the way it sounds).

Fav places to hang out: Taco Bell, Red Robin's, dance clubs in downtown Portland, football games.

Fav things kids here do with free time: Participate in school sports or activities (cheerleading, dance team, band, drama, etc.), work part time, hang out at friends' houses, rent movies, see laser light shows at the planetarium, hang out at the waterfront on the Willamette River. Also, skiing is very popular.

Issues heavy on our minds: Budget cuts in schools, the possibility of no more school sports or activities, class size increases due to lack of money for teachers.

Can't-live-without clothing for guys and gals: Levis jeans, hiking boots, Converse All-Stars, T-shirts with sports-related logos ("Nike is especially popular because it started here"), white socks, anything from the Gap.

The future looks: " . . . like a struggle to reach success. Twenty-five or 30 years ago, all you needed to get a job was a high school diploma, but now you have to have a college degree and post-graduate work, and even that doesn't guarantee you anything."

Our heroes: Sports figures, teachers, youth group leaders; people find heroes in their everyday lives.

Teens at our school worry most about: Drinking—"One of the most stressful things we have to deal with is peer pressure to drink alcohol." Also, getting accepted at good colleges, money, getting good grades/SAT scores, dating, getting into trouble with parents, STDs, pregnancy.

Weirdest things students at our school do: Streak pep assemblies, set off stink bombs in school hallways on a regular basis.

AMPHITHEATER HIGH SCHOOL

Tucson, Arizona

Student body type: 2,000 students, grades 9 through 12. Very diverse, mostly Hispanic and black. Whites are the minority here.

Favorite music performers: SWV, Jodeci, Dr. Dre, Bell Biv Devoe, alternative, R&B, top 40—Cypress Hill to Garth Brooks.

Most fab food: Grandma Tony's Pizza.

Fav places to hang out: Little Anthony's (a 1950s diner), Golf 'n Stuff (miniature golf, go-carts, batting

cages, arcade), malls, dance clubs.
Fav things kids here do with free time: Sleep, hang out with friends, party, cruise the streets, play sports.
Issues heavy on our minds: Sex, AIDS, and the fact that most people are having sex but not using condoms though they know the consequences. Also, fights ("they're common in our school"), racial tensions, violence, weapons, drugs.
Can't-live-without clothing for guys and gals: Girbaud, Guess (for the white crowd); Cross Colours (for the black crowd); Dickies overalls, slacks, and big jackets (for the Mexican crowd); also, baggy clothes or the prep look, plus a range of unique clothing.
Teens at our school worry most about: Grades, college, social acceptance, sex, relationships, independence, money.
The future looks: Challenging—"A lot of us know what we want and that it's not going to be easy to get it."

WILSON HIGH SCHOOL
Wilson, Kansas
Student body type: Very rural. About 130 students, grades 8 through 12; all white. Mostly college-bound.
Favorite music performers: Ranges widely, but most like Alabama, Def Leppard, and Pearl Jam.
Most fab foods: Mexican and pizza.
Fav places to hang out: Our local convenience store (Mighty Mart 2) or older friends' houses.
Fav things kids here do with free time: Party! Most drink alcohol on weekends. Some play sports.
Issue heavy on our minds: Alcohol abuse.
Can't-live-without clothing for guys and gals: Comfortable jeans.
The future looks: Difficult—"We're all pretty ready to approach it, but most think it looks pretty rough. Most students haven't ever experienced big-city life, so a big adjustment is ahead."
Our heroes: Older students, famous athletes, and other people who have done great things with their lives.
Teens at our school worry most about: Getting the grade, alcohol, keeping fit and looking good.

FOR BETTER OR WORSE . . .

Veteran Teachers on How Today's Teens Are Different From Their Parents' Generation

FOR BETTER:
"In some ways they're a little sharper than we were."

FOR WORSE:
"I think they read less. They see a lot of things firsthand, like Operation Desert Storm, and I think those things are powerful influences on them. I think they grow up too fast. I wish they could be children a little longer."

—**Barbara Clark, Jefferson Middle School, St. Charles, Missouri,** phys. ed. teacher who has taught since 1963

FOR BETTER:
"I think the kids are more tolerant of differences than they used to be. They are more accepting of other kids who aren't in their cliques than in the past, though I can't say bigotry has disappeared. Also, teenagers today are more likely to question authority, which has its good side. As a teacher, you like the kid who challenges some of the things you say. In some ways it's good that kids are less inhibited about their position and more comfortable about speaking up."

FOR WORSE:
"They are much more apathetic, with much less respect for authority. Kids are into doing their own thing. They're not so much interested in the corporate ladder. They know they're going off to college, but for most kids there's no concern about building a resume to get there. There's a top level of kids who are in sports, have a ten-hour-a-week job, work hard at school. But that group of students is not as big as it was. The apathy is the most frustrating thing."

—**Tom Howard, Walt Whitman High School, Huntington Station, New York,** social studies teacher who has taught since 1965

FOR BETTER:
"For the better, I'd say they're a little more inquisitive—'show me, prove it to me, give me more information so I can check it out

and see if you're right'—in a good sense. They're asking about things we didn't ask about that perhaps we should have been asking about."

FOR WORSE:

"Students aren't nearly as self-motivated as they once were. There's a real drop-off in their vision of the positive possibilities that lie out there for them. The family life they come from is so much less structured, less supportive. That has really made it a lot tougher for them."

—**Jay Stricherz, McIlvaigh Middle School, Tacoma, Washington,** principal, teacher/administrator for 21 years

---

FOR BETTER:

"They're more informed at a given age. They have insights into things at earlier ages. So you can deal with issues and concepts with many of the students earlier than you once could have—in a positive way—which opens up some opportunities for instruction."

FOR WORSE:

"I think teenagers today expect instant entertainment—all information should be entertaining because MTV is. They want the informational benefits of any school experience to be instant. That means there's a dissatisfaction with what many of us [parents and educators] see as traditional ways of moving yourself through life—gaining knowledge, for example, or preparing for the future. Deferred gratification is a concept most adults today understand—this is a little difficult for today's teenage generation."

—**Sandy Addis, Anderson School District One, Williamston, South Carolina,** veteran high school guidance counselor, now director of special projects

---

FOR BETTER:

"Whether this is a good thing or not, I don't know, but one thing I noticed when I started teaching in Harlem in 1968 and 1969: They looked poorer. You used to see kids in their father's hand-me-down pants and shoes. You don't see kids dressed that poorly anymore. The total economic prosperity seems to have increased, though you have to wonder if the source of it isn't more welfare and illicit income from drug dealing."

FOR WORSE:

"What all the teachers [in my school] are saying is the students seem to have less academic ability than in the past—not that they were so great in the past, but there was always a handful of better kids trying their hardest. We don't have the bright kids we did before. They're just not as skilled at reading and math. Also, they don't seem to be worried about anything. In my generation, more kids were worried about achieving and having a good career. These kids are more laid-back. They're smoking a lot of marijuana. Some are smoking crack occasionally. They drink; there seems to be more of that. They don't seem to be worried about financial matters, though there are a lot of kids working 30, 40 hours a week. That's why they don't study or do homework."

—James Hackett, Bronx, New York, social studies teacher who has taught since 1968

Walkin' the Walk, Talkin' the Talk

Style is at least as important as substance for teenagers. Whether it takes the form of outrageous hair color or audacious tattoos, teens are always looking for new ways to declare their individuality. At the same time, they're notorious clique-joiners, with a yearning to belong. It's all about a sense of identity.

TEENSPEAK TRANSLATED

Move over, "awesome." Even "phat" is almost old hat. Here come just some of the latest and greatest words dotting the landscape of American teenage language:

PROPS = compliments, appreciation for achievement
MAP PROPS = the highest compliments
DOG = Hey, you. "Hey, dog." Also, a guy who sleeps around.
FLUFF CHICK = airhead
CRUSTY = guys' term for a girl who is repulsive
FRONTING = putting on a front
PLAYER = a guy who always has a different girlfriend

CONVERSATION WITH A GIRL WITH GREEN HAIR

The place is a busy street in New York City's Greenwich Village. A young girl strolls by, not unlike many others strolling by—except for one thing. She has green hair. The time is fall 1993, as work is commencing on this book. I can't help but stop and ask her more than a few questions.

Her name is Katy Kroll. She is 18, from Boston, and a freshman at nearby New York University.

Q: You have lovely long green hair. How come?

A: Because green's my favorite color and I want to stand out.

Q: How long have you been green?

A: About a year now.

Q: Did you wear it this way at your high school?

A: Yeah.

Q: What kind of high school did you go to?

A: I went to the Boston Latin School . . . an [entrance by] exam school. My class was filled with 300 preps, and I was the only quote unquote *liberal* person in my class. I won "Most Liberal." For Halloween I dressed up as a prep. I wore loafers, I tied my green hair back, and everybody died. They just stopped in the hall. And the captain of the football team asked me out that day and said, "Are you going to be like this forever?" And I said, "No." And I came in on Monday and looked normal [with green hair flowing and prep accoutrements gone], and [the guys] took back all their offers.

Q: What did your parents say?

A: Um . . . my mother actually liked it. My father never said anything. He still hasn't said anything.

Q: How is your green hair being received at college?

A: It's good because people can pick you out of a crowd really easily. And let's see, I've gotten "Katy, Katy, the green-haired lady" as a nick-name. "Katy the green-haired bimbo" is another name. And they just go, "Katy has green hair"—that's how they describe me. Anyone can find me.

Q: Did anybody of authority ever ask you to change it?

A: Not for school, but on job interviews. I was turned down for a job in a bagel shop, but I did have a job for six months scooping ice cream in an ice cream store, and my boss loved my green hair.

Q: So it doesn't seem to have many "cons," and it has a lot of "pros"?

A: Yeah, well . . . I can't blend. Like, I can't just go somewhere and not have people stare at me. Sometimes it gets annoying. People walk down the street, they're like, "Hey, you have green hair." Really? I didn't know that. Or, "Does it *grow* like that?" I thought, I'm going to come to New York and nobody's going to pay any attention to me, but they go, "Hey look, she has green hair!"

Q: So it's not a political statement?

A: No. I dyed my hair pink once—but I decided I hate pink. I had to pick another color. So I thought, Gee. What color would really stand out? And I was like, green! I've met a couple other people with green hair, and they think we're spiritually connected for some reason. They try to talk to

SCAMMER = someone who isn't committed to one person and has a lot of boyfriends or girlfriends
HOOCHIE= a girl scammer (see above)
SPLACK = sexual intercourse
STUNTS = sex
SLACK = sexually loose
DIRTY = weird or abnormal. In some parts of the country this means *good.*
IT'S ALL REAL = "It's cool."
FILTHY = cool
FREAK = attractive. "She's so freak."
HERB = a loser; someone who tries hard to be in a certain crowd but doesn't cut it
ZEKE = like a herb (see above)
DITCH = to skip school
GAT = gun
GLOCK = gun

ZINE = magazine
PC = politically correct
GETTING UP = putting your graffiti "tag" or symbol in public view
HAT, JIMMY HAT = condom
WANKING = putting on airs; also, copping out
NOSHING = making out
MACKIN' = making out
REPRESENT = to put your best foot forward, stand for something strong and positive, make a showing
GETTING BUSTED = getting grounded by parents
RAGE = to party hard
BUFF = muscular
RANDOM = bizarre, strange
HEINOUS = ugly
HEIN = a shortened version of heinous (see above)

me, but I don't really want to get into a conversation with them. And when I came to NYU, the first week I was there I dyed three people's hair different colors. They were like, "Do you use Manic Panic?"—which is the kind of hair color it is. And I'm like, "Yeah." And they said, "I've got a bottle of blue. Would you like to dye my hair blue?"

Q: Can you imagine a time when you won't be green anymore?

A: I can't. I don't know what I'm gonna do 'cause I've had it for so long. Last night I was [saying to some friends], "I think I'm going to dye my hair back to the natural color. The entire room turned around and went "Huuuuh?! You *can't* do that! How are we going to find you? You have the only green hair."

Q: What's your major?

A: I'm majoring in music. Vocal performance. And minoring in politics. And just for the record, I'm gonna be famous some day. I'll be on MTV.

The time is an hour or so after our conversation. I am walking through Washington Square Park in the center of Greenwich Village. I spot my newfound friend Katy (not hard to do). She is sitting with a friend who has magenta hair. Honest.

PICK OF THE CLIQUES

From band geeks to drama jocks, from herbs to tree huggers, from druggies to wannabes . . . teens may detest cliques, but they can't escape them. Adolescent culture has a long history, and cliques have been a prominent part of it going back to ancient Greece. Experts say cliques serve a critical psychological role at a time when young people are struggling to make the very important transition from the family to independent adulthood. Within a group of like-minded peers, teens find a place to try out new roles and try on new identities. While parents sometimes don't like the group their teens fall in with, psychologists say young people are usually drawn to cliques whose members share their interests—whether they be sports, music, shopping, academic achievement, or rebellious behavior. Teens with similar personal problems often hang together too.

Jocks and Preps

In the social hierarchy of American high schools and middle schools, the jock is still king. Sports are *huge* in most places. And teenage sportsmen and sportswomen are much admired by their fellow students.

There are still preps too, and plenty of 'em. The difference between preps and jocks, at least in some places, is that preps care a lot more about clothes and their appearance than jocks do. Preps are most likely to be found in Gap and J. Crew clothes. They're academically oriented, concerned about college and careers. They're not likely to do drugs, though drinking is commonly part of their scene. They often have money and nice cars.

CHEESY = corny, stupid
KICKS = shoes
FRESH DIP = casual dress
GRUBBIN' = good food
HIGH POSTAGE = high maintenance
CHOLO = macho
BOOT = to throw up
PIMP = sarcastic term for a guy who gets around
FIST IT = shut up
CHIQUITAS = women, girls
JACK = rob
LAID-BACK = well dressed
TWO-FOUR = a six-pack
40s = 40-ounce cans of malt liquor
9 = 9mm gun
FRYING = taking LSD
DROP = LSD

In case you've been living in a cave:
AWESOME = great, unbelievably great
PHAT = cool
FLY = cool
BUSTED = uncool. The opposite of "fly" (see above).
WORD! = the 90s version of "right on"; indicates agreement with another's remark
DISS = to disrespect, dismiss, drop or dump someone or something
DEF = cool

Skaters, Bikers, et al.

Special interests, especially sports, can be the rallying point for cliques. Skaters, bikers, surfers, and snowboarders are consumed by their sport and are easily identified by their slang, their favorite music, and the clothes they wear. Some teens say skaters are out of style or are a middle school phenomenon that falls away once teens get their driver's license. But skaters and bikers remain prominent cliques at some schools, and you can recognize them by their long hair (long all over or shaved short in back with long bangs, or dreadlocks), baggy pants or shorts, and T-shirts with skateboard-company logos. In coastal areas, you'll find surfers too—forever tanned, forever blond, forever barefoot, forever at the beach. And where the weather permits, you'll also find the new kids on the clique block: snowboarders. Somewhat similarly dressed are taggers—graffiti crew members—who are usually found in more urban areas.

Stoners, Burnouts, Druggies, et al.

Stoners—also known as burnouts, bangers, druggies, or dirtbags—survive too. With their (sometimes sensitive and poetic) dark moods, dark clothing, dark-themed heavy metal music, cigarettes, and, sometimes, drug and alcohol abuse, they affect a "who gives a crap" attitude. Teens at some schools report that this group can also include seriously troubled kids. (Explains one suburban middle school teacher, "They do coke and grass, sniff Wite-Out, and 'shroom [take hallucinogens].')

Long Live the Nerds

Nerds and brains are the supersmart: on the one hand derided by some of their fellow students, on the other admired in a generation that knows intelligence can help you get ahead and get all the material goodies you want later on in life.

Alternatives

More recently emerged are the alternatives, who take on different characteristics from school to school but share some attributes across the board. For the most part, alternatives want to be just that—different from everyone else. They can dress simply—in flannel shirts and jeans, with chokers for the girls—or, like latter-day hippies, they might wear long skirts and sandals. They can also be more extreme, dying their hair pink or green and wearing only dark colors or colors and patterns that don't match. They usually favor alternative music too. In some places, the alternatives also smoke cigarettes, drink coffee, and do drugs.

In some schools, the alternatives may also include freaks, though freaks may be even more extreme—"punk without the leather," as one teen described them. Hippies, a term you hear now and again, can fall into this clique category, as do Deadheads (Grateful Dead fanatics) and tree huggers—environmentally concerned types who may also sport the hippie look their parents remember.

"Among the preps you'll find the cheerleaders, goodie-goodies, do-gooders, and student government types," says Patricia Howard, a teacher on the freshman campus at Smithtown High School in Smithtown, New York. Within this group you'll also often find the snobs. The snobs will talk to kids from other groups—but only when their friends aren't around.

"Not every teen can be so readily pegged as a member of this or that clique," says Marian Salzman of BKG Youth. "Mainstream kids—those who aren't trendsetters—are particularly apt to form circles of friends that are only loosely affiliated with a clique 'type,' most notably preppies and jocks. It's clear to which groups these kids *don't* belong," she says, "but they don't make much of an effort to identify themselves as members of the group to which they *do* belong."

Ravers

Ravers can look either like alternatives or skaters, which covers a lot of ground. Their lives are ruled by music, especially techno, and the dance club scene and all-night rave parties that surround it. They live for the weekends and the chance to groove to the music (and sometimes the illegal substances) central to this scene. They tend to be found more often in college circles, but there are a number of teens—particularly in big cities—who identify themselves as ravers too.

Wiggers and Wannabes

Surely the most curious blip on the clique screen is the wannabes—or wiggers (a contraction of "white" and "nigger"), as they are also called. *Newsweek* recently termed them "white B-boys in the burbs"—mostly suburban guys and girls who adopt a black or sometimes Hispanic attitude. While they're certainly out there in large numbers, many schools have no teens of this type at all. Students at schools that have wannabes often say they're perplexed by the phenomenon.

Wiggers and wannabes take it to the extreme, walkin' the walk and talkin' the talk. You can usually tell them by their baggy pants, back-turned caps, headphones, just-out-of-the-joint gait, and high-five jive. For some it's a political statement, an expression of solidarity with other cultural groups. For others it's just the generations-old teenage desire to emulate musicians they admire. For still others it's a way to be different, to get noticed. Or it can be a rebellious rejection of their own culture's values.

And for a small number it's an attempt to find *some* group to fit in with. Whatever their motivation, wiggers and wannabes are often looked down upon both by the group they're aspiring to join and by teens of their own kind. But don't tell *them* that. They think they're cool.

TEEN FASHION

You can't figure it out. You want them to wear pretty things, or at least jeans that don't have holes in them. You beg, you plead, you buy them nice stuff that hangs in the closet or sits neatly folded on a shelf. You have forgotten what *you* looked like at their age—your hair out to here or down to there, jeans so tight you could hardly breathe, homemade jewelry, oddball shoes. You are stumped by what you see walking into your local high school in the morning or stepping out your own front door. Girls wear guys' boxer shorts in place of more standard bermudas, or "Daisy Dukes" so tight and short you want to wrap a blanket around them. Guys wear shorts so big, so baggy, they look like part of a circus act. And today's teens have a penchant for piercing themselves. All over. They do things with their hair that were unimaginable during your teen years—and dying it pink is the least of it. They leave the house looking like someone from another culture, another planet. (Parents with a prep or a jock in the house may have an easier time of it, as these cliques tend to go mainstream Gap and J. Crew.)

Herbs and Posers

Herbs and posers aren't cliques, exactly. They're individuals trying very hard to be part of cliques or to be something they're not—perhaps metal heads, hip-hoppers, skaters, or wannabes. Herbs and posers adopt the fashion, slang, and musical tastes of the group to which they aspire, picking up parts of the look but never quite getting it together.

"A herb is different from a nerd," says 16-year-old Rebecca Cohen of Stuyvesant High School in New York City. "If a guy is hanging with a crowd he wants to be with and tries very hard to fit in and fails, he's a herb. Someone who's a nerd is actually more respected because that's their life and they're not trying to be something they're not."

In a generation of teens that places high value on being "authentic," you *don't* want to be called a poser or a herb.

Psychologists say clothing choices teens make are part of the group-identifying behavior that comes with the adolescent transition from the family to adulthood. Clothing is a way of showing you fit in and indicating exactly which group you belong to. Or it's a way of expressing your individuality. What teens wear sends an instant message—I'm a prep, I'm a druggie, I'm a gangster, I'm unique.

For more troubled young people, clothing extremes not seen in the school community say either "I dare you to take me on" or "I don't belong here." Among teenagers, appearance is a major deal. Wear the wrong sneakers and even your best friends (and this happens among guys too) will tear you apart. Teens take their clothes and appearance very seriously. Parents should know this, lest a teen's clothing choices create battles that need not be.

What Teens Want vs. What Parents Want

How do teens want to look? "Girls want to be fashionable but also attractive to the opposite sex," says Adriane Butler of Philadelphia-based Urban Outfitters, a chain with more than 15 stores in cities and college towns nationwide. "They're influenced most by each other. They're also influenced by musicians they admire, film stars, and what they see on the streets. Guys are the same way with skateboarding gear and surf gear." Guys also want to be attractive to girls, she adds.

"I think parents want their kids to look respectable, going to school clean and organized. Kids just want to be creative, and sometimes being creative isn't always being organized, neat, and functional," Butler continues. "I think parents should support that. If kids weren't creative, Donna Karan and Calvin Klein wouldn't be doing what they're doing. For so long Donna Karan did wrap skirts and sarongs; recently she brought out sports looks and other kid-inspired ideas."

Mary Clarke, creative director of *Sassy* magazine, adds, "On the one hand some of them want to look really, really individual; on the other there are some who just want to fit in." Clarke finds that girls who are very interested in fashion dress for themselves and their friends, not to please boys.

Clarke believes the hippies of the 1960s, with their long hair and wild clothes, exhausted many of the parent-irritating looks. "Now the only way you can annoy your parents with the way you look is with tattoos and earrings," she explains.

The Shape of Teen Fashion

Comfort and value are two driving forces in teen fashion today. The hip-hop homeboy look has been making way for "work wear": big canvas jackets, overalls—"the real thing," according to Clarke. This makes denim a major fashion item, according to Sasha Charnin Morrison, senior fashion editor at *Seventeen* magazine. "In the world right now, everybody wants to be casual and feel comfortable," she says. "Teens see their favorite people—on TV, on albums, on magazine covers—wearing jeans.

Rest reassured, teens *do* care what their parents think (well, up to a point, anyway). "It's amazing when trying on clothes in a department store or mall on a weekend how often you hear teens in the next dressing room say, 'My mom would *kill* me if I bought this,'" says Sasha Charnin Morrison of *Seventeen* magazine. Morrison shares a memory from her own teenage years that she thinks might help parents who feel their teens are turning into fashion nightmares. "As a teenager, I used to spend a lot of money on makeup and hair products," she says, "and I would experiment with them—especially hair colors, rinses, and home perms. It's not that you need any of it, it's just that

you're so eager to grow up quickly, and this is the time to experiment. When I did, my mother realized it was just a phase and left me alone. My parents sat silently by. Though it probably wasn't easy for them, that was the best thing they could have done. If they had said, 'You look horrible,' I probably would have done more. I probably would have rebelled. I *didn't* do drugs. I *did* ruin my hair."

All the big models wear them. Denim is a universal, affordable fabric, and because it fits a lot of different body types well, it's the perfect 'security blanket' during the awkward teenage years." Also very big with this generation of teens is vintage clothing—and even guys like the retro flavor of the thrift-store look, according to the Zandl Group, a New York–based marketing consulting firm specializing in the teen market.

"Everything is going pretty slim," Morrison says. "You can't hide anything anymore. There are peg-legged pants. The school-girl look. Everything is very youthful. It makes everybody feel young, fresh, and sexy." Urban Outfitters' Butler sees teens gobbling up shrunken child-size T-shirts to wear with jeans or under a shirt, sweater, or vest. "And let's face it," she adds, "they can wear it."

Teenagers want to look different from their parents, says Butler, and that's not as easy as it used to be. With middle-aged people taking better care of themselves and looking and dressing much younger today—leggings and all—teens "really have to do some stuff that's extreme," she explains.

Teen fashion experts and teens themselves seem to agree that a cleaner, more natural look is what teens want now. Less makeup. Less pretense. Pony tails. Headbands. Caps for "bad hair days." The simple sports shoes of the 60s and 70s, like old-style Adidas and Pumas. Or "retreads"—used clothing that's usually inexpensive, often well made, and sure to give a teenager a one-of-a-kind look.

Pardon Me, But Isn't That an Earring in Your Eyebrow?

Want to make your parents *really* nuts? Get your body pierced. "For rebelling adolescents, piercing is the ultimate Mohawk," said *Newsweek* in 1993, referring to the 1980s shaved-head-with-a-swath-of-hair-down-the-middle punk hairstyle.

"My mom cried. She was really disappointed in me," says an attractive 16-year-old girl from Dix Hills, New York, with a hint of regret in her voice and a small silver ring in her nose. "I finally had the guts to do it," she adds, summoning a measure of pride. Though she has only had a pierced nose for two months, she feels she will still be wearing a nose ring when she's 50.

Body piercing is partly about having the guts to do it, partly about being different (different takes a lot more these days), and partly about fashion. Among the pierced and famous are Axl Rose of Guns N' Roses (nipple ring), fashion model Christy Turlington (pierced navel), and countless other stars of music, modeling, movies, and sports.

Some teenagers—yikes!—do body piercing on themselves. For a more "professional" job, they can find piercing emporiums in most major cities (and many smaller ones). The Gauntlet, for instance, is a chain with shops on both coasts. At its New York store, an eyebrow-piercing job recently cost one teen $30 plus the cost of a gold hoop.

A centuries-old practice with a rich and diverse cultural history, body piercing can go too far. Six pierced earrings in one ear, two in the other—

Shoes, Glorious Shoes

Footwear is a very big deal in a teenager's life today. Just ask Nike. Or Reebok. Or Timberland. Irma Zandl, president of the Zandl Group, a teen-focused marketing consulting firm, found that shoes are among the top items teenage girls collected in 1994 (along with clothes, poems, and CDs). Says Mary Clarke, creative director of *Sassy* magazine, "We probably get more calls and mail-in requests for information on where to buy shoes than anything else. Young people will go to the ends of the earth to find a pair of shoes they like."

Fashion Hazards

When you were a teen, you may have worried about getting sent home from school because your skirt was too short or your hair was too long, but that was probably where your dress code problems ended. Today's teens have to worry about whether they might inadvertently wear a color or article of clothing with a gang connotation or an item for which they could be mugged or worse. In Atlanta, for instance, backpacks are no longer allowed in some schools since they might conceal a weapon. (As a result, see-through backpacks of clear vinyl or mesh are now popular all over.) Baggy jeans are

that's nothing these days. A pierced eyebrow, a pierced tongue, a pierced navel . . . all are, yes, commonplace. And sometimes they're all on the same person. If your teenager comes home looking more and more like a loose-leaf binder, it's probably time for a chat.

Tattoos: Not Just for Sailors and Hell's Angels Anymore

And, of course, there are tattoos. No, not the wash-off "impostors," but the for-life commitment to a rainbow on your daughter's shoulder or a winged heart on your son's biceps. Tattoos are more popular with teens today than ever before, culture-watchers say. "Really, it's an absolute explosion," internationally known tattoo artist Ed Hardy told *Newsweek* in 1991. "What's counterculture gets melted down and utilized by the rest of society." And only more so in the past several years.

Adults deserve at least part of the blame, should you wish to place it somewhere. The older generation, particularly celebrities and twentysomethings (many of them professionals), have embraced this form of body decoration in a major way, making it something for younger people to emulate.

Cher, for example, had six tattoos by one recent count. Supermodels Stephanie Seymour and Carre Otis are just two members of the fashion set who wear theirs proudly. Basketball star Shaquille O'Neal sports a modest Superman-style "S" on his left upper arm. Scottie Pippin of the Chicago Bulls has one. Dennis Rodman of the San Antonio Spurs reportedly has nine. Also among the much-ballyhooed tattooed are Tom and the ex-Mrs. Roseanne Arnold, Julia Roberts, Johnny Depp, Jody Watley, Jon Bon Jovi, members of the Indigo Girls and Motley Crue, and oh so many others.

While tattooing is still banned in some American cities, the number of professional tattoo "studios" has ballooned in the last 20 years, from a few hundred to an estimated several thousand now. In Miami there's Lou's Tattoos, among several others. In Tucson you can find the Enchanted Dragon, Hidden Dreams, and Ancient Art Tattoo. Teens say that any college town is a good bet if you're in the market for a tattoo—or body piercing.

Tattoo artists take their work extremely seriously, and some say they make it a policy not to tattoo drunks or anyone under 18 unless accompanied by an adult. Still, teens find a way. But what about a way out?

For the most part, tattoos won't come off no matter what you try—rubbing 'em out, burning 'em out, slicing 'em out, freezing 'em out. And while dermatologists are aiming new laser technology at tattoos with some promising results, these treatments can add up, both in terms of cost and time. It's not a one-visit-and-it's-gone deal. And so far there's no guarantee they can *un*tattoo you.

banned in some California schools because they, too, may be used by students to hide guns and knives. T-shirts with violent, sexy, sexist, or pro-drug messages are also prohibited in many schools. Beepers and cellular phones (a hot item among teens, though sometimes the accessories of drug dealing) are now banned in some districts because they are considered too disruptive. Large, flashy pieces of gold jewelry are also "uncool for school," making young people targets for trouble. And school administrators report that with the popularity of bustiers and meshy see-through tops for girls, overly revealing outfits have become another major fashion headache.

Love and Sex: Risky Business

Romance remains a constant feature of teen life, no matter how much times may change. A date for the prom. Love notes passed between classes. A summer love. Four-hour phone calls. All these are still part of the scene. But love, like so much else, has become more complicated for today's teens. "Dating"—or whatever today's teens choose to call it—often means flirting with danger.

Reasons for Dating Someone for the First Time

(Teenage boys and girls ages 14 to 19)

	Guys want	Girls want
Good personality	68%	75%
Good looks	66%	59%
Intelligence	40%	36%
Good body	39%	24%
Sex appeal	36%	14%
Popularity	9%	8%
Money	3%	3%

Source: Love and Sex in the 90s Survey, 1991, conducted for *Seventeen* magazine by Market Facts, Inc.

DATING—THE WORD, ANYWAY—MAY BE OLD HAT

There's something very weird going on out there, parents. Its existence emerged innocently enough, from a question I posed to dozens of teens from coast to coast: "What word do you use most that parents understand least?" From California to New York, from Iowa to Florida, came the reply: "dating." *Dating?* Seemed pretty straightforward to me. But according to teens, "dating" is what older people and parents do. Even "going out" doesn't mean what it used to. New terms have been devised. New meanings are being applied. Here are some translations of the latest terminology, as explained to me by a group of New York City–area teens.*

Stage 1—"Kickin' it." It goes like this: You say hello to someone, introduce yourself, or otherwise get a conversation going. The person can reject you or "kick it back."

Stage 2—"Talkin' " or "rappin'." This is when you're in the phone-calling stage and meeting in social places where there are other people around.

---

*Thanks to Audrey Ince, Matthew Alacardi, Jennifer Ahn, Cenophia Mitchell, Andrew Ronan, LiLi Brown, and Joe Rodriguez.

Stage 3—"Seeing each other." (This is where parents *really* get confused.) "Seeing each other" means hanging out with no commitment. There could be sex at this point, but not usually.

Stage 3A (optional)—"Hitting." Sex without commitment. Applies only to some.

Stage 4—"Going out" or "going." Doesn't actually mean going *out* anyplace. You could be staying at home together. This brings a whole new dimension to the age-old question, "Would you like to go out with me?" But anyway . . . the final stage of going out is taking the person to family occasions. That's when you know it's serious—in the old-fashioned sense. Whew!

Instructions for parents: Discuss this with your teenager. It should be good for a few laughs. And you still won't understand it when you're through.

Trauma-less, Drama-less Dating

It is a typical Saturday night at the Steak 'n Shake across from the Galleria shopping center in Brentwood, Missouri. One of the movies showing at the mall's multiplex theater is not long over. Fifteen young teens are crowded around a string of pushed-together tables, partaking of burgers, fries, and another popular teenage pursuit: the group date. Especially among younger teens, dating in groups is the way to go—and go out—these days. Teens report it's a great way to explore relations with the

Favorite Dating Activities

According to the Kodak/BKG Youth American Teens, American Dreams survey, the typical date involved dinner or a movie or both, according to 53 percent of respondents. Next in popularity was hanging out with a group of friends, cited by 46 percent. (Interestingly, one-third considered dating more of a group thing than a couple thing.) Only 7 percent of the sample chose something cultural to do on their dates. Also, the study declared, "The prom is still a major focus of attention. Fully half the sample thought of the prom as 'maybe the most memorable night of my high school years.' "

In Your Face: Sex Facts

By their twentieth birthday, 41 percent of white women and 63 percent of nonwhite women will have been pregnant at least once.

Most of the increase in female sexual activity in the 1980s was among white teenagers and those in higher-income families, narrowing the previous racial, ethnic, and income differences.

60 percent of sexually active women ages 15 to 19 report having had two or more sexual partners.

Source: Facts in Brief: Teenage Sexual & Reproductive Behavior, The Alan Guttmacher Institute

opposite sex and share activities and interests. Gone is the pressure to have sex—to the relief of both girls and boys. There's just one drawback: If you get involved with someone in the group and then break up, look out. Not only do you lose the relationship but you could lose the whole group and have to find a new crew to hang with.

Sex in the Age of AIDS

Birds do it. Bees do it. Teens do it—at younger ages, in greater numbers, and with more partners than ever before. According to the latest available figures from the Alan Guttmacher Institute—a leading source of statistics on reproductive behavior—27 percent of unmarried young women and 33 percent of unmarried young men have had intercourse by age 15. By age 19, 75 percent of women and 86 percent of men have had intercourse. Even compared with the sexually liberated early 1970s, these numbers are *way* up.

One striking aspect of sex among today's teens is the ever-younger ages at which they are having it—sometimes just out of elementary school, teachers and principals report. Teens are, very simply, more sexually sophisticated and more provocative in their dress and behavior than teens of generations past. Another striking fact, according to researchers: Even wealthier white girls who once would have waited until marriage—or at least until college—to have intercourse are waiting no more.

What's Love Got to Do With It?

What factors influence teens when it comes to having sex? The number one influencing factor was "peer pressure and popularity" for 30 percent of teens surveyed nationwide in the Teen Lives: 1992 Teen Attitudes Survey conducted by BKG Youth. "Lust" was right up there too—a motivating factor for 29 percent. "Curiosity" prompted 24 percent to try sex. So what about love? Just 16 percent of those surveyed said love influenced their decision to have sex. "Drinking/drunkenness" was cited by 12 percent.

What's AIDS Got to Do With It?

Despite the well-publicized risks of contracting the HIV virus through unprotected sexual contact, AIDS doesn't have very much to do with sex for a great many teens. They *say* they're worried. They get tested for it. They ask potential partners to do the same. And then? Among high school students who are currently sexually active, fewer than half—only 45 percent—reported that they or their partner used a condom during their last intercourse, according to a 1990 report by the U.S. Centers for Disease Control.

A Cavalcade of Partners

Monogamous relationships are not necessarily the order of the day. By ninth grade, according to a 1990 CDC report, 19 percent of boys had already had sex with four or more partners. As California's notorious Spur

In Your Face: AIDS Facts

- **AIDS is now the sixth leading cause of death among young people ages 15 to 24.**
- **Of teens who are sexually active, fewer than half reported using a condom the last time they had intercourse.**
- **The number of AIDS-infected adolescents is doubling nearly every 14 months.**

Source: U.S. Centers for Disease Control

Teens Speak on AIDS and Sexual Practices

(excerpts from interviews with Washington, D.C.–area teens)

"There was one time I had sex and it was unprotected. I didn't think about it at the time—I was caught up in the moment. Now it's always in the back of my mind: Will that be the one time that gives me AIDS?"

—June,* 15

"I think it's really sad. I don't care how caught up teenagers are in the moment. Protecting yourself is just what you have to do. That way you don't get pregnant, either."

—Brenda,* 16

Posse proved last year, it's still cool among the guys to keep score. What about the girls? According to the latest figures available from the Alan Guttmacher Institute, in 1988, 27 percent of girls ages 15 to 17 who reported having had intercourse had done so with four or more partners. Since the late 1960s and early 1970s, the Guttmacher Institute reports, the proportion of sexually experienced girls ages 15 to 19 reporting having had only one partner declined from 62 percent to 39 percent.

Out of the Closet in Middle School

Today's teens must take a stand on sexual issues—and define themselves sexually—at increasingly younger ages. Bisexuality is in, say teens from coast to coast. Gay and lesbian rights are hot issues in school newspapers. *Roseanne*'s "lesbian kiss"—introduced by a parental advisory—aired in prime time in 1994. A week later, an HBO special, *More Than Friends: The Coming Out of Heidi Leiter*, aired as part of the *Lifestories: Families in Crisis* series, telling the story of a teenage lesbian who takes her girlfriend to the prom.

Condoms? In School?

Condom distribution in schools is a hot topic, not just for teens in big cities but for those in the tiniest burgs.

In small towns, "the only stores that sell condoms are little general stores," explains 16-year-old Stacia Potter, who attends Hampshire Regional High School in the quaint and quiet community of Westhampton,

Massachusetts. Stacia believes condoms should be available in school for those who want them. "If a boy went into one of these stores to buy a condom, it would be all over town," she notes. "This is part of what makes it an issue for students here."

While parents and school boards battle it out on the issue of condom distribution, polls of teens show the majority are in favor of it. According to the 1993 CNN/*USA Today*/Gallup U.S. Teens Poll, close to 60 percent said they thought "machines that dispense condoms should be placed in our school." Similarly, BKG Youth's 1992 Teen Lives Survey found that 67 percent of teens believe their schools should distribute condoms.

What's a Parent to Do?

"If there's a parent who finds it easy to talk with their teenager about sex, I think we'd all like to meet that person," says Laurence Steinberg, Ph.D., professor of psychology at Temple University and co-author with Ann Levine of the book *You and Your Adolescent* (HarperPerennial, 1990).

Steinberg says that when he speaks to groups of parents and kids about sex, it's usually the parents who are reluctant to have the conversation, not the kids. "Kids wish parents would talk to them about sex," he says. "Parents need to know this. Secondly, parents need to know that communicating with your child about sex won't make your child more likely to have sex. There's a lot of good research on this. What it does do is make kids behave more responsibly."

"There's big-time sex experimentation going on among teens," says Matthew Alacardi, 19, of Queens, New York. "It's chic and trendy to be bisexual and be 'out' about it. You find 14-year-olds saying, 'I'm bi' or 'I'm gay'—coming out not only to their friends but to their families. It's ridiculous to me to label yourself at such a young age. But because of Madonna and movies like *The Crying Game* and things on TV, it's definitely happening."

Information Please

Where do teens get most of their information about sex? A 1993 *Time*/CNN poll conducted by Yankelovich Partners asked them. Most younger teens, ages 13 to 15, got their information from their parents (30 percent), followed by friends (26 percent), school (26 percent), and entertainment media (15 percent), *Time* reported in May 1993. As teens got older, the survey showed, friends became the primary source of sex info—among 16- and 17-year-olds, friends edged out parents 37 percent to 22 percent. School was cited by 15 percent in this age range; entertainment media was cited by 18 percent.

Steinberg believes there is no one correct message parents can give teenagers because parents differ in their own values and beliefs. "It's key to feel comfortable about expressing what you believe, and that will make communication much more open and honest," he says. "If you believe your son or daughter shouldn't be sexually active during these years, you should say so—and say why. Just issuing a dictum won't work." Kids at this age need your explanation.

"On the other hand," Steinberg continues, "it's also fine for a parent to say—if the parent believes this—'You're 16, you're in a relationship with someone you care about, and if you decide to have sex, here's what you should be thinking about—AIDS, pregnancy, responsibility, ethics.' To be an effective parent, you don't have to start from the position that sex is bad. You can be a good parent even if you think it's okay for children to be sexually active once they reach a certain age." Steinberg adds, "I think hearing this will be a relief to many of today's parents."

Some Teens Say: Not Now, Later

More relief for worried parents: While sex may be on every teen's mind, some are pledging not to make it part of their immediate futures. They're jumping on the "True Love Waits" bandwagon of sexual abstinence until marriage, a program developed by the Southern Baptist Convention and embraced by a number of other religious groups.

"Abstinent teens seem thrilled to know how many hundreds of thousands of their peers share their values and have made similar promises to abstinence until marriage," says Richard Ross, spokesman for the "True Love Waits" campaign. "Also, teenagers seem happy to discover that there is a group of adults who have not given up on them and who believe teenagers are fully capable of making promises and keeping those promises."

Teens by the tens of thousands from coast to coast have signed the following pledge: "Believing that true love waits, I make a commitment to God, myself, my family, those I date, my future mate, and my future children to be sexually pure until the day I enter a covenant marriage relationship."

TEEN PREGNANCY—WHAT'S NEW NOW

Pregnancy is a big worry for today's teens, as it was for most of their parents during *their* teenage years. But contraceptives are important for more than one reason these days: Having sex without condoms can also carry with it the risk of contracting the AIDS virus or other serious sexually transmitted diseases.

One thing pregnancy doesn't carry with it for teenagers now is the same measure of shame and social stigma it did in previous generations. While a great many teens and parents still disapprove of pregnancy in the

"When I was in high school, girls got pregnant and they disappeared," said Richard Schuldt of Eau Claire, Wisconsin, in the *New York Times* late last year. "Now, my pregnant daughter goes on *The Montel Williams Show.*" Schuldt's daughter April became the center of controversy—and an outpouring of student support—when her election as homecoming queen was challenged by school administrators because she was five months pregnant. The school officials were later disciplined.

In Your Face: Teen Pregnancy

- **One out of every ten teenage girls ages 15 to 19 becomes pregnant each year in the United States—approximately one million young women annually.***
- **By age 20, 44 percent of young American women have been pregnant at least once.***
- **Births to unmarried teens have jumped dramatically in the past 20 years. In 1970, fewer than one-third of all teenage girls who gave birth were unmarried, compared with almost two-thirds in the early 1990s.****
- **While teenage pregnancy rates among blacks are nearly twice as high as those**

teen years or before marriage, support for youngsters who do become pregnant and want to have the baby appears to be gaining, especially among their peers.

At a mostly black high school in the Midwest, Imani,* a senior who is at the top of her class, told me teenagers with babies are not uncommon in her school. "It's their choice," she said of classmates who are pregnant or already mothers. "For me, it would be a tragedy."

Nowadays, pregnant girls and new mothers are "mainstreamed" in many public schools. In some places, school-based day care for their infants is also available. Part of the change is the belief that keeping these teens in school is preferable to having them drop out, perhaps never to learn the skills they need to become gainfully employed. Another part of it is a 1972 federal law that makes it illegal for schools receiving federal funds to expel students or prevent them from taking part in school activities either because they are pregnant or because they are parents. And while some schools may try to skirt the regulations, teens themselves are challenging school administrations now.

Last year, when several cheerleaders became pregnant and were ordered off the squad by the school board in the small farming town of Hempstead, Texas, a furor erupted. Many students and parents demanded that the pregnant girls be allowed to continue in their cheerleading roles. The community's moral dilemma played out in the headlines and on the networks. A major national organization threatened a lawsuit. The school reversed its decision.

The birth rate among unmarried teens has increased dramatically in the past 30 years, and many parents, students, and officials worry that support of pregnant teens sends the wrong message. Because so many of these births occur to young women living at or below the poverty level, adolescent pregnancy is at once a health, moral, and economic issue.

"When I think of all the girls I know in school who are pregnant right now or have babies, it really scares me," says Melissa Vink, an 18-year-old senior at Pella Community High School in Pella, Iowa. In this church-going town, where the high school student population numbers about 500 (85 percent white and 15 percent Asian), Melissa can, without hesitating, tick off the names of ten girls in her school with babies newly born or on the way.

"Everybody says this is something they wouldn't want to happen to *them,*" adds Melissa, who identifies herself as a Christian and says she doesn't believe in premarital sex. "But once the girls get pregnant, they're not treated badly. Their friends are pretty cool with it."

No matter what your view on the subject, the growing acceptance of teenage mothers (and fathers) by their peers and in their schools is just one of the new facts of life for teenagers in the 1990s.

among whites,* the relative *increase* in births to unmarried teens has been much greater among white girls than among blacks in the past two decades.**

Sources: *The Alan Guttmacher Institute
****The National Center for Health Statistics, U.S. Dept. of Health and Human Services**

How Teens View Abortion

American teenagers seem to be even more divided than adults on the question of abortion, according to a Gallup Youth Survey. Asked to pick one of two extremes on the issue, 47 percent of teens surveyed in 1991 said they favor allowing abortions for any reason, while 44 percent of teens said they support outlawing all abortions.

What Becomes of the Baby?

Teens who become pregnant today almost always either have an abortion or give birth to the child and raise it themselves. Only about 3 percent of never-married white women and 1 percent of never-married black women put their child up for adoption, according to the latest available figures.

Source: Sex and America's Teenagers, 1994, The Alan Guttmacher Institute

WATCH IT, BUSTER

As the line has blurred between assault and "typical" youthful male sexual advances toward girls, the rights—and strong reactions—of today's young women are coming into sharp focus.

Pinched, tickled, or forced up against the wall in the hall, teenage girls (many of whose mothers were told as teens to "be flattered" or "let it slide" when the same things happened to them) today tell harassers to "buzz off" (and worse) or sometimes use physical force to repel unwanted behavior. Battered girlfriends are emerging from behind dark glasses to bare their bruises and report their abusers to school officials and police.

In schools today, students who want to fight back have the force of federal sex discrimination law (Title IX) behind them, as well as legal precedent in the form of recent court damage awards to teens whose schools failed to take sufficient action when harassment was reported.

A Problem That Runs Silent, Runs Deep

In May 1993, *Seventeen* magazine published results from a major nationwide survey on sexual harassment in schools, conducted in conjunction with the NOW Legal Defense and Education Fund and the Wellesley College Center for Research on Women. The responses follow:

- An astounding 89 percent of young women said they had experienced sexual harassment at school within the past 12 months.
- 83 percent reported being touched, pinched, or grabbed.
- Close to half said they had been leaned over or cornered.
- Nearly 40 percent said they were being harassed on a daily basis during the past year.
- 27 percent reported pressure to do something sexual.
- For 10 percent, harassment meant being forced to do something sexual (some reported being assaulted or raped).

Almost all the harassment came from fellow students; 4 percent of respondents reported situations involving teachers, counselors, administrators, or other school staff. The NOW Legal Defense and Education Fund reported being told of a teacher in a New York school who said to a student, "I'll give you a 96 if you give me a 69."

Reactions to Harassment

- **Telling the harasser to stop was the number one reaction girls reported, though many said they had also walked away.**
- **40 percent said they had resisted with physical force.**
- **13 percent said they did nothing.**
- **Most told someone, either a friend (66 percent), a parent (18 percent), or a teacher (18 percent).**
- **When students did tell a teacher or administrator, schools took action 55 percent of the time.**

Source: *Seventeen* magazine survey

At Work and at Play

Working part time and participating in sports have traditionally been two of the most parent-pleasing ways teens spend their free time. But as juggling school and a sometimes heavy work schedule becomes increasingly common, experts worry teens are suffering from *overwork* and missing out on their youth. Meanwhile, physical activity is taking a nosedive among all but the athletic elite.

"Last year, Veronica Vega was getting A's and practicing the clarinet two hours a day. But then, like millions of other American high school kids, she began working—afternoons, evenings, weekends—not because she needed to but because she wanted to. Now she pays her own phone bill and car insurance, but that's not the only way she's paying. This year Veronica got her first F."
—*Life* magazine, July 1993

AT WORK . . .

Jobs are now a major force in teenage lives. As many as two-thirds of high school juniors and seniors and half of all sophomores hold some kind of job during the school year. One-third of teens who have jobs report working more than 20 hours per week.

Where the Money Goes

Some teenagers *must* work; they have a parent out of a job, a family to help support. But numerous studies show that most teens are working because they *want* to. For frills. In one 1991 study, just 6 percent of high school seniors surveyed said most of their earnings were going to help pay family living expenses; only 10 percent said they were saving most of their earnings for college. As for the rest? Well, let's face it: Teens have things to buy—clothes, shoes, cars, stereo equipment, CDs, home video games, concert tickets, more shoes, vacations.

Risk vs. Reward

A part-time job has long been viewed as a terrific character-building and maturing experience for a young person. But career-enhancing, apprentice-like work is now largely a thing of the past, replaced by more routinized, fast-paced, service-type jobs for teens. And experts studying the teen work trend aren't so sure about the benefits anymore—especially when weighed against emerging risks.

According to Laurence Steinberg, Ph.D., professor of psychology at Temple University and a leading researcher in adolescent development, "There is now a broad consensus among educators and scholars that working more than 20 hours per week—especially in high-stress jobs—puts teens at risk for trouble in school and out."

In a 1993 study, Steinberg and his colleagues found that taking on a job for more than 20 hours a week served to "diminish youngsters' investment in school, increase delinquency and drug use, further autonomy from parental control, and diminish feelings of self-reliance." After one year of working, the study found, "previously nonemployed adolescents who had been working more than 20 hours weekly were using drugs and alcohol 33 percent more often than their counterparts who had remained unemployed."

The Bottom Line

While kids say they love the extra spending power work provides, teachers see the strain on their faces and in their test scores. Extracurricular activities like sports, band, or drama club—an enriching part of teenage life—fall by the wayside. Often, so does homework.

The bottom line for parents, Steinberg says, is rethinking the number of hours a teen works. "A job held for ten hours a week may give your child

What Field Do Teens Want to Go into When They Grow Up?

MALES

1977	1991
1. Skilled labor	1. Business
2. Engineering	2. Computers, electronics
3. Law	3-5. Law, Sports, The arts (tie)
4. Teaching	6. Medicine—physician
5. Sports	7. Skilled labor
6. Music	8. Engineering
7. Architecture	9-11. Auto repair, Architecture, Law enforcement (tie)
8. Farming	
9. Medicine—physician	
10. Military	

FEMALES

1977	1991
1. Secretarial work	1. Nursing
2. Teaching	2. Teaching
3. Nursing	3. Medicine—physician
4. Medical technology	4. The arts
5. Veterinary medicine	5. Business
6. Modeling	6-7. Law Communications (tie)
7. Medicine—physician	8. Science
8. Social work	9. Veterinary medicine
9. Business	10. Child care
10. Cosmetology	

Source: America's Youth in the 1990s, George H. Gallup International Institute, 1993

the potential benefits of working—extra spending money, a feeling of being more grown-up, of getting out in world—without jeopardizing her school and her health," he notes.

BILLION-DOLLAR BABIES: TEENAGE MEGA-CONSUMERS

Does it sometimes seem to you that teenage tastes, styles, interests, and sensibilities are driving the *entire* commercial marketplace? If so, it's with good reason. Teenagers are *big* spenders. As consumer groups go, this one is, well, awesome.

Consider this: In 1953 there were 17 million teenagers who spent $7 billion annually, according to the Rand Youth Poll, a New York–based marketing research firm that has studied teen trends for more than four decades. Now there are an estimated 25 million teenagers spending a whopping $61 billion each year, according to the organization's 1993 Rand Youth Poll on Teenage Economic Power. Add to that the $24 billion parents give them annually for family grocery shopping, plus the $127 billion in influence young people have on other products purchased by parents, plus the $10 billion teens say they're saving for the future, and, the poll found, the total teenage impact on the national economy is approximately $222 billion. Yep, teens control $222 *billion* in consumer spending. No wonder you can't get them to clean up their rooms.

How Teens Spend Their Money

And on what, you wonder, are they spending their hard-earned bucks—and yours? The poll found some answers here too. Among girls ages 13 to 15, for instance, clothing leads the list. Next comes spending on food, followed by movies and entertainment. Among boys in this age group, food and snacks are number one. Clothes rack up second place.

Like younger teens, girls 16 to 19 spend first and foremost on clothes. Food and snacks come second. Then come cosmetics. About 11 percent of their spending money is saved, most of it for costlier purchases later on, the poll revealed.

Among boys 16 to 19, food and snacks take the biggest bite out of their spending budget. Boys this age say 20 percent of their earnings and allowance is saved, most of it for more expensive purchases later on such as cars, stereo equipment, and electronics.

Spending Battle of the Sexes

In more than 40 years of tracking teenage spending, girls have consistently outspent boys every year, says Lester Rand, president of the Rand Youth Poll. "This is largely because girls are far greater impulse buyers than young men, visit stores more often, are more socially involved, have less consumer resistance (especially when it comes to sales), and have a

Inside the Teenage Pocketbook

Boys 13-15
Weekly allowance: $16.15
Weekly earnings: $15.85
To spend weekly: $32.00

Boys 16-19
Weekly allowance: $30.15
Weekly earnings: $45.20
To spend weekly: $75.35

Girls 13-15
Weekly allowance: $19.35
Weekly earnings: $17.85
To spend weekly: $37.20

Girls 16-19
Weekly allowance: $32.45
Weekly earnings: $50.00
To spend weekly: $82.45

Source: Rand Youth Poll on Teenage Economic Power, 1993

Teens' Favorite Participation Sports

Here are the sports teens participated in during the past 12 months, ranked in order of popularity. (Note: Numbers add up to more than 100 percent because some teens took part in numerous sports.)

Sport	Percent of teen participants
Basketball	56%
Swimming	50%
Bicycling	47%
Jogging	46%
Football (touch)	45%
Football (tackle)	43%

high fashion and fad consciousness, all of which contribute to their spending propensity. Also, girls list shopping as one of their primary activities; boys frequently resist this pastime," Rand explains.

Living in a (Somewhat Less) Material World

For all their vast spending power, today's teens appear to be moving away from the "material world" Madonna sang about in the 1980s, a recent survey found.

"Teens' switch from materialism to social concerns is the most dramatic finding in a ten-year review of their behavior and attitudes," according to Peter Zollo, president of Teenage Research Unlimited, whose Northbrook, Illinois, firm has been studying the teen market in depth since the early 1980s.

Only 32 percent of teens surveyed in 1993 agreed with the statement "success means making a lot of money," compared with 61 percent just four years earlier.

AT PLAY . . .

School sports are a big deal in most places. Make that a *huge* deal. To a great many teens, sports matter more than *anything*. After a loss in a crucial game, the biggest, brawniest varsity tackle weeps openly with his teammates on the field—along with classmates and parents in the stands. The fortunes of whole towns rise and fall with a high school team's performance in any given year. The guys and girls who are top athletes in their schools are major heroes to their peers. To get that way, they work out, work at it, and practice, practice, practice.

A Lot of Talk, Not So Much Action

But how active are *most* teenagers? Not very, according to the most recent figures available from the U.S. Department of Health and Human Services/Public Health Service. Just 37 percent of students in grades 9 through 12 report being vigorously active (for 20 minutes or more) three or more times per week. Guys are far more likely to take part in regular vigorous activity than girls (50 percent vs. 25 percent). Of ninth through twelfth graders in 1990, well under half—43 percent—played on one or more varsity or junior varsity teams at school.

The Older They Get, the Less They Do

As teens get older, their involvement in regular vigorous activity drops off. The drop is sharpest among girls: from 31 percent in ninth grade to 17 percent by grade 12. Among the boys, 51 percent take part in vigorous physical activity in grade 9, while 44 percent do so in grade 12. In 1984, according to the U.S. Department of Health and Human Services, 62 percent of students in grades 10 to 12 reported participating in vigorous

Weight training	**43%**
Regular fitness program	**42%**
Bowling	**41%**
Fishing	**36%**
Tennis	**34%**
Roller skating	**31%**
Soccer	**30%**
Softball	**28%**

Source: America's Youth in the 1990s, George H. Gallup International Institute, 1993

Teens' Favorite Spectator Sports

	Males	Females
Football	49%	33%
Basketball	18%	25%
Baseball	12%	13%
Hockey	5%	3%
Tennis	1%	5%
Soccer	—	4%
Volleyball	—	4%
Wrestling	2%	1%

Source: America's Youth in the 1990s, George H. Gallup International Institute, 1993

physical activity. In 1990, only 36 percent of students in grades 10 to 12 said the same.

For all the attention today's adults pay to getting fitness activities into their own lives, teens appear to be turning away from physical pursuits in large numbers.

"It's very clear there are a lot of groups that were left out of the fitness boom," says Dr. Michael Pratt, a medical epidemiologist with the U.S. Centers for Disease Control in Atlanta. "Kids are one of them."

Sensory Overload

Music,

TV, video games, computers—all are a huge part of teens' lives today, shaping the way they dress, the way they talk, the way they think. Music videos flash all kinds of crazy images into your home and into your teen's brain. Beavis and Butt-head have replaced Beaver Cleaver and his brother, Wally, as a new generation's heroes. While teens eat it up, parents and experts worry. Yes, violent imagery and sexual explicitness abound in lyrics, TV shows, and videos. But it's not all senseless sensationalism; there's some really high-quality stuff out there, some of which parents might even enjoy if they gave it a chance. Herewith a reluctant traveler's guide to the world of teen media, intended to help you sort out the good from the bad from the downright ugly.

Teens Speak on Music

"I think adults are more worried than they need to be about rap music and MTV. If the kid is really a good kid, the music isn't going to turn him around."
—Anna Blumenthal, 14, the Dalton School, New York City

"My brother listens to all that gangsta rap music. It doesn't disturb me. I like the beat."
—Tiffany Wallace, 17, Rayen High School, Youngstown, Ohio

FROM ROCK TO RAP—AND EVERYTHING IN BETWEEN

Long the driving and unifying force among American teenagers, music is one tough bailiwick for their parents. Especially today. Between gangsta rap and heavy metal, teens listen to music that could (and does) send their parents screaming to psychiatrists and other experts for advice. And not without reason. Some of today's biggest, hottest, best-selling music stars—not just alternative, metal, and rap musicians but mainstream rock and pop artists too—sing songs promoting casual sex, glorifying drug use, and denigrating women. By any measure, the use of vulgarities in lyrics today is extreme.

Efforts to label, censor, and lighten up some of current music's heaviest and deadliest themes continue. (And parents need note: While censorship efforts have produced less sexist, less sexual, less violent, less offensive versions of *some* rap and metal songs for radio play, what you get on an album can be quite another story.) Meanwhile, lawsuits brought by stricken parents of teenage suicides against performers and their lyrics have met with little success in the courts. And it is true that millions of teenagers listen to such music without killing themselves or anybody else. How you feel about the music teens listen to today—and efforts to obscure or obliterate it—depends on how you feel about the First Amendment and the free speech rights it guarantees, a subject that won't be argued here.

So . . . check your complaints and censorship arguments at the door. The stuff is out there. Your teens buy the records or hear them at a friend's house or on the radio. They see the music videos—if not at home, then elsewhere. If they're like most red-blooded American kids, they know the tunes—though quite often not the words. And when they do finally figure out the lyrics, many teens are as outraged as you are.

How you feel about today's music is something you might want to talk about with your teen. But *listen* to some before you speak or you'll have no credibility on the topic whatsoever. You may find you don't object to *all* of it. Maybe you even *like* some of it. Experts say discussing how you feel—and why—is a way to instill your values in your children and help them listen and think more critically about this and other matters.

Consider what follows a Baedeker to today's teenage music scene. And remember, *your* parents went nuts when you listened to the Rolling Stones.

METAL

They look scary. They sing about scary stuff. Satan. Suicide. Heaven and hell (hell, mostly). Decadence and death (death, mostly). They give

METAL DETECTOR

You can almost always tell a metal album by its cover. You're most likely to succeed by looking for the following symbols: skulls, skeletons, crucifixes, daggers, lightning bolts, occult symbols, and, oh yes, barbed wire.

Listen Your Way to a Cultural Clue

For a quick overview of metal music, Geri Miller, executive editor of *Metal Edge* magazine, offers the following dozen suggestions from metal's long history.

Metal Classics

1. **Led Zeppelin—*Zeppelin IV***
2. **Guns N' Roses—*Appetite for Destruction***
3. **AC/DC—*Back in Black***
4. **Aerosmith—*Permanent Vacation* (or *Toys in the Attic*)**
5. **Motley Crue—*Shout at the Devil***
6. **Black Sabbath—*Vol. 4***

themselves names like MegaDeath, Slayer, Anthrax, Napalm Death, Slaughter. They dress in (at least as far as parents are concerned) hideous clothing and wear horrifying hairstyles. They pierce every visible body part (and some that aren't visible) and hang metal ornaments anywhere they can. They probably don't have an easy time of it at airport security. They snarl, they scowl, they scream. They make parents completely crazy. They laugh all the way to the bank.

They are the heavy metal musicians teenagers—and some adults—just adore. And the more parents are stumped, stymied, and steamed by these performers and the music they make, the more teens love it.

It's true: Some of the things they sing about may not be exactly what you want your child listening to—sometimes frightening, sometimes outrageous, depending on your perspective. You will find, for instance, avowed Satanists and other kinds of extremists in the mix (Deicide, King Diamond, and Cannibal Corpse to name just a few). The stage antics of the most extreme groups—which *they* claim are satire—can be pretty shocking. Self-mutilation and bloodletting are not uncommon stunts among the more outrageous groups. But most often, metal performers sing about rebellion and antiestablishment themes, always popular with teens. Actually, metal music as a genre has mellowed and broadened since the late 1980s. Some of metal's biggest names—Metallica, for instance—have crossed over into more mainstream musical and lyrical themes.

Metallurgy 101: A Crash Course

Here's a mini-guide to metal music and some of its forms. While some bands fall firmly into one category, many start out as one type and cross over or cover a variety of styles on the same album.

Traditional heavy metal. Compared with its successors, thrash metal and death metal (see below for definitions), traditional heavy metal has been described as "conservative." Song-based, with "great riffs" critical to this and other metal forms, it's described by its fans as melodic and powerful, with aggressive guitar plus up-front, sometimes operatic-sounding vocals. It can take its themes from Dungeons & Dragons–type fantasy or be earthy, rebellious, or reality-based.

Death metal. This is the metal music parents find most worrisome. "Death metal is the most extreme form of music known to man; heavy metal at its most violent and intense, at its fastest, meanest, and ugliest," write music journalists Paul Elliott and John Hotten in their book *The Best of Metal* (Collins Publishers, San Francisco, 1993). "As the genre has evolved, the music has grown ever more brutal and obscene as each new band attempts to top all previous excess." It's really extreme stuff, though extreme sells in all kinds of genres for all kinds of reasons.

Thrash. Now considered passé, thrash has been called "the ultraviolence of the mid-1980s." "Thrash was normal guys wearing their normal clothes, playing complex, fast, musically heavy music," says Katherine Ludwig, editor of *Metal Maniacs* magazine, adding, "It made you bang

7. Kiss—*Alive*
8. Def Leppard—*Pyromania*
9. Judas Priest—*Unleashed in the East*
10. Metallica—*Metallica*
11. Bon Jovi—*Slippery When Wet*
12. Ozzy Osbourne—*Tribute*

Ultimate heavy metal bands include: Judas Priest, AC/DC, Iron Maiden, Def Leppard, Deep Purple.

Ultimate death metal bands include: Deicide, Venom, Morbid Angel.

Ultimate thrash bands include: Metallica, Megadeth, Anthrax, Slayer.

Ultimate pop metal bands include: Bon Jovi, Poison, Nelson, Slaughter.

Other bands that are sometimes labeled metal but are actually hard rock include: Aerosmith, Guns N' Roses, Led Zeppelin, Van Halen, the Black Crowes.

Ultimate groove groups include: Pantera, White Zombie.

Ultimate grindcore bands include: Napalm Death and other bands on the Earache Records label.

Ultimate industrial metal groups include: Prong, Ministry, Helmet.

your head, hair flying. You just had to." Metallica, which crossed over to mainstream hard rock in the early 1990s and has consistently written songs relevant to kids' lives, started off as a thrash band, featuring thrash's characteristic heavy riffing. Still, some thrash groups serve up fare parents would find quite offensive.

Pop metal. These bands, whose biggest fans are 13- to 15-year-old girls, tend to cultivate a nonthreatening pretty-boy image. This more lightweight version of heavy metal is big on melody, with easy-to-take lyrics. Pop metal is mostly slow, mainstream love songs with up-front guitar. Long hair and powerful, hard-edged guitar make it more metal than pop.

Glam. Painted faces, tousled hair, and high-heeled boots are the trademarks of this outmoded but nostalgically remembered rock-rooted metal-image music. Alice Cooper started it all in the early 1970s. The New York Dolls, Hanoi Rocks, and Kiss followed suit. Motley Crue rode the glam look into the 80s, followed by Poison, but apparently success gives way to cold cream—both Motley Crue and Poison have long since dumped the look. Glam, which every so often threatens to make a comeback, remains good for a few decent tunes and a few good laughs.

New Directions in Metal

Groove. "It's cleaner, simpler, yet I wouldn't call it conservative," says Marina Zogbi, associate editor of *Metal Edge* magazine. Groove often appeals to non–metal heads. You can recognize it by repetitive musical themes. "It's a groove you can really get into," says *Metal Maniacs* magazine editor Katherine Ludwig; hence, perhaps, the name.

Grindcore. Another type of music apt to make parents cringe, grindcore has been described as a blur of abrasive sound. "It was supposed to take up where death metal left off as the newest, most extreme form of metal; however, no one is really sure what the difference is," says Zogbi. Adds Ludwig, "It can be very extreme-sounding, like it's almost not even music, with people playing superfast and not always doing it well." What puts grindcore in the realm of death metal is guttural vocals.

Industrial metal/noise metal. This is usually a cold, repetitive, machine-like sound, often using "samples"—bits of sound injected from prerecorded sources. It's music of a more experimental nature, by performers who came out of an artsy, urban, avant-garde scene. It tends more toward the noisy than the melodic. Some groups, like the nonindustrial MegaDeath, have had songs remixed with an industrial twist (but don't confuse it with industrial, which is not metal but more in the realm of techno; see upcoming section).

ALTERNATIVE

Alternative has become the broad term for any kind of music that's anti-mainstream. Alternative music is no one type of sound. It could come

In the beginning (a couple of years ago), alternative meant recording on a small independent label, being noncommercial, being undiscovered by the masses. So once a group hits it big, the term alternative is something of a misnomer. Now, alternative is a Grammy category.

An infamous feature of many alternative music concerts, even some by the mellowest pop-type groups, is the mosh pit. Once a prominent part of the punk music scene, the mosh pit is the area in front of the performers known for producing blood, bruises, and broken bones when crazed fans scramble on stage and jump into the crowd below.

Grunge, **as in the ubiquitous fashion trend, is a word that comes from the muddy, sludgy guitar sound typified by bands like Soundgarden and Nirvana. "The sound came first; then followed the bands, who happened to live in Seattle, where it's chilly and where wearing flannels, long underwear under cutoffs, and caps just makes sense," says music journalist Marina Zogbi, associate editor of *Metal Edge* magazine. "These bands started out not trying to look like anything. Then suddenly, fashion designers brought out grunge lines. So the groups started wearing jeans and T-shirts instead." And grunge went from "in" to a dirty word.**

from Britain, from Seattle, from Ireland. It could be country or folky. It could have a rock, a metal or a hippie vibe. In terms of the Pacific Northwest's homegrown grunge sound, it's a case of heavy metal meets punk.

If there's a unifying element in alternative music, it's attitude—anti-capitalist, anti-authority, anti-conformity, and anti-big business and the nine-to-five work culture. It frequently advocates doing your own thing. Though sometimes quite mellow, alternative often evokes dark themes, with lyrics about the inner struggles of the misunderstood, the misfit, the outsider, or the tortured intellectual who finds the world a horribly lonely place for anyone who's sensitive or different. All of it has a lot of appeal for teens. The life, lyrics, struggle with drug addiction, and ultimate suicide of Nirvana lead singer Kurt Cobain reflect the inner turmoil, angst, and alienation so often heard in this musical genre.

Alternative groups also tend toward political correctness, seeming more sensitive to women than many rock bands, with their overtly sexual lyrics and videos. You will, however, also find alternative lyrics promoting sexual behavior or drug use or rhapsodizing about death and suicide.

"Alternative is simply a trend," says Mordechai Kleidermacher, managing editor of *Circus* magazine. "A lot of groups felt it wasn't 'in' to be metal anymore, so they put on flannel shirts and ripped jeans, shaved their heads, and grew little goatees to fit into it." Kleidermacher believes some very big rock and metal groups are now looked down upon because they were flashy, glitzy, and outwardly mass-oriented in the 1980s.

"Alternative is supposedly more personal," he says, "but deep down inside I think everyone wants to sell records. I think the alternative bands are just more neurotic about it. They talk about feeling guilty about their success instead of feeling happy about it."

Alternative musicians take pride in making it the hard way, singing from the heart, putting their integrity above everything else. "Eddie Vedder [of Pearl Jam] is very popular because he emits this aura of integrity and complains that the group got too popular," Kleidermacher says. "He talks in interviews about kids growing up nowadays and how they have a really hard time being accepted by their parents. He appeals to the lonely teenager in all of us."

COUNTRY

It's big with teens. Very big. And getting bigger from coast to coast. No gangsta country or thrash country performers have emerged to raise parental concern—yet.

A Beginner's Guide to Alternative Performers

Nirvana
Pearl Jam
Smashing Pumpkins
Alice in Chains
Stone Temple Pilots
Blind Melon
White Zombie
Nine Inch Nails
Rage Against the Machine
Live
Candlebox
Soundgarden
Mudhoney
The Pixies
The Cranberries
The Breeders
Beck

Belly
Depeche Mode
The Cure
U-2
Liz Phair
P.J. Harvey
Juliana Hatfield
Phish
Violent Femmes
Soul Asylum
Thrill Kill Kult
Lemonheads
The Butthole Surfers
Primus
Porno for Pyros
Dinosaur Jr.
Gin Blossoms
. . . and so many more

TECHNO

"Mindless, brainless dance music that gets you sweatin'" is the way one teen described the music that accompanied Britain's rave explosion in the 1980s and was incorporated into the American dance-till-you-drop rave scene that followed. Techno, also known as trance in its more danceable form, began as a hard-core, beat-driven, heavily electronic sound found strictly in dance clubs and DJs' collections, but it has expanded to include mellower music to veg out by, known as ambient techno. Also popular is jungle, which merges the hard-driving techno beat with hip-hop and reggae. While still not the kind of fare most teens would buy to listen to at home, it's the ticket for those looking for a groove in which to move.

RAP UNWRAPPED

You can't stand it. You can't *under*stand it. You thought, you hoped, you prayed it was going to go away. You could not have been more wrong.

Call it hip-hop, call it rap, but whatever you do, call it *big*. Because that's what it is. *Very* big. It is the beat of this generation of teens, as popular in the most upscale suburbs as it is in the inner city.

Rap—hardly a new phenomenon—has been around since the mid-1970s. Spawned by street-corner DJs in some of New York City's toughest neighborhoods, rap began as a danceable alternative to disco. Rap's first commercial hit was "Rapper's Delight," by the New York–based Sugar Hill Gang, in 1979. Now the music is performed by artists straight out of Compton and straight out of comfortable suburbs—blacks mostly, though you'll also find some Latinos and occasional white rappers. Rivalries between New York rappers and L.A. groups (which often have a harder edge) flare from time to time.

Parents may know rap music for lyrics they find detestable. But while they may consider rap's message frighteningly violent and frightfully sexist, young people often see rap music as profound social commentary.

"The main thing that comes through in rap is anger, regardless of the lyrics," said Todd Gitlin, professor of sociology at the University of California, in the *New York Times* late last year. "No matter [what] your background, young people across America have something to be angry about, and rap allows them to express that anger. It's the beat, the lyrics, the percussion, the boom, boom, get out of my face."

Although for lots of fans it's just a beat, just something to dance to, to many teens it is the poetry of modern life, a reflection of conditions that exist and need to be noted. If you look at the music in this context, they say—if you listen to it with an ear for the content and a heart open to the language of lives led in conditions beyond your worst imaginings—you

In 1993, $780 million worth of rap records were sold, according to industry figures. More than half of the purchasers were age 17 or under. Of those, 50 percent were between the ages of 10 and 14.

Rap is "the great rock 'n' roll of its day . . . rich with all of the qualities that have always made rock 'n' roll great: big beats, sex, wit, humor, nonsense, adolescent rebelliousness, grown-up revolutionary sloganeering, wild haircuts, cool clothes, and more sex," according to aficionado Bill Adler in the book *Rap* (St. Martin's Press, 1991).

may arrive at the view that rap music, especially in its most extreme forms, is simply an example of medium as message.

And, it seems, the more violent the message—and the messenger—the more it sells. When gangsta rapper Snoop Doggy Dogg was arrested in connection with a murder in 1993, he made headlines and zoomed to the top of the charts. His then just-released album, *Doggystyle,* sold more than three million copies in just a few weeks. Rappers who initially enjoyed success in the commercial mainstream, like Hammer and Kris Kross, tried to make comebacks in 1994 by adopting a tougher image and a harder lyrical edge. Gangsta sells. The more authentic, it seems, the better.

Critics of the genre counter that it's a bunch of talentless young people trying to get rich by exploiting violence and vulgarity while inciting a generation to shoot, plunder, and kill.

Critics particularly take issue with the likes of Ice-T, whose controversial song "Cop Killer" helped make him famous. And Sister Souljah, whose lyrics drew fire from President Clinton when he was a candidate. And 2 Live Crew, the king of obscene rappers, whose album *Nasty as They Wanna Be* was deemed legally obscene by a Florida judge in 1990. And Public Enemy, who have been called "the most aptly named group in the history of rap."

Delores Tucker, chair of the National Political Congress of Black Women, has been an advocate for banning gangsta rap on obscenity grounds. Testifying before the Senate Subcommittee on Juvenile Justice in February 1994, she explained that her group is not against rap or hip-hop and that it supports "the artistic creativity of our young people." However, she noted, her organization believes gangsta rap and "the misogynist lyrics that glorify violence and denigrate women are nothing more than pornographic smut" that, she told the senators, "coerces, influences, encourages, and motivates our youth to commit violent behavior, use drugs, and abuse women through demeaning acts."

But when it comes to rap, offensive is sometimes in the ear of the beholder. Says Kate Ferguson, editor in chief of *Word Up!* and *Rap Masters* magazines, "For black people, Public Enemy could be considered a 'good' group—pro-black and socially aware—though to some, especially in white society, their language and imagery might seem scary in terms of their message about black people doing whatever is necessary to stand up for themselves and equality. As for sexually explicit rap lyrics," Ferguson adds, "they're no different from what you find in men's magazines sold on newsstands."

One of the most notorious rap albums ever made is *Nasty as They Wanna Be,* by 2 Live Crew. In his book *Learn to Discern* (Zondervan/HarperCollins, 1992), Bob DeMoss Jr., a former DJ who is now a youth-culture specialist with Focus on the Family in Colorado Springs, Colorado, outlines what you'll encounter in this recording (which, incidentally, sold more than a million and a half copies):

- 87 descriptions of oral sex

Rap Sheet

Here's a guide to some of the major rap performers to help parents figure out who's who and what's what. Some are "good," meaning their lyrics are *not* particularly objectionable. Some are "not so bad"—or at least not all the time. And some, by the standards of most parents and a good many teens, are just plain "ugly"—an assessment gangsta rap performers are only too flattered to hear.

This list was compiled with the help of teenagers from Los Angeles, Youngstown, Ohio, and New York City, and with the expert assistance of Kate Ferguson of *Word Up!* and *Rap Masters* magazines.

The Good

De La Soul
SWV
Queen Latifah
DJ Jazzy Jeff & the Fresh Prince
Hammer (the "old" Hammer)
Jodeci
A Tribe Called Quest
Arrested Development
The Puppies
Ahmad
Monie Love
Kid 'N Play
Doug E. Fresh
Kool Moe Dee
Souls of Mischief
Fat Boys
Main Source
P.M. Dawn
Special Ed

- 117 explicit references to male and female genitalia
- 226 uses of the "f" word
- 163 uses of "bitch" when referring to women
- 81 uses of the word "sh—"
- 42 uses of "ass"

Despite all the controversy it engenders, rap music has retained its vitality, musicality, and popularity—as suggested by such acts as SWV, De La Soul, Brand Nubian, Arrested Development, A Tribe Called Quest, Digable Planets, and many others. It's a multibillion-dollar business, with artists who win Grammy Awards and—the ultimate sign of mass acceptance—get invited to the White House.

Rap Styles

- **Pop rap.** Nonthreatening rap with crossover potential. Pop rap is music the public at large will not find threatening or offensive. Pop rap artists include: DJ Jazzy Jeff & the Fresh Prince, Vanilla Ice, Marky Mark, De La Soul, Kid 'N Play, Hammer (his earlier recordings).
- **Culturally militant/Afrocentric rap.** Lyrics having to do with black pride, cultural history, and awareness. Also, politics: standing up for your rights, "being willing to go the whole nine" to change things—even if it means violence—not being satisfied with the status quo, building black businesses, aiming for economic autonomy. Culturally militant and Afrocentric rappers include: Afrika Bambaataa, Public

Enemy, Professor Griff (after his split from Public Enemy), Nefertiti, Brand Nubian, Sister Souljah.

- **Sexually explicit rap.** This is the stuff that makes parents crazy. These rappers include: 2 Live Crew, Luther Campbell, Too Short.
- **Gangsta rap**. Another source of parental uproar; often a combination of machismo, violence, and sexual explicitness. Women are objects, and there's a lot of boasting about what they're good for; there's even the occasional rating of female body parts. Plus a lot of bragging about what guys can do—their physical prowess, their potential for violent or deadly action. Gangsta rappers include: Snoop Doggy Dogg, Wu-Tang Clan, NWA, Dr. Dre, Ice Cube, Ice-T, Just Ice, Schoolly D.
- **Latin rap.** Very much a part of hip-hop culture, to which Latinos have contributed musically and culturally from the beginning—though black artists got most of the fame. Latin rap performers include: Mellow Man Ace, Kid Frost, the Latin Alliance, Cypress Hill.
- **Frat-boy rap.** "Do what you want to" and "let's party" themes with appeal to the white college crowd. Frat-boy rap performers include: the Beastie Boys, Big Men on Campus.
- **Cautionary rap.** Speaks of the importance of education, staying off drugs, positivity in the community, the high cost of getting a "rep" (reputation) in the neighborhood, taking responsibility when you have

Whodini
Heavy D
Kris Kross
Chubb Rock
Digable Planets
Boyz II Men
Young MC
Mary J. Blige
En Vogue
Salt-N-Pepa
Kool Herc
Afrika Bambaataa
Gang Starr
. . . and many more

The Not So Bad

Roxanne Shante
EPMD
LL Cool J
Beastie Boys
Big Daddy Kane
Domino
Brand Nubian
Eric B. & Rakim
Sir Mix-A-Lot
Slick Rick
Bel Biv DeVoe
MC Lyte
Naughty by Nature
Das Efx
Yo-Yo
Boo-Yaa Tribe
Biz Markie
Run-DMC
Tone Loc
. . . and many more

sex or father a child, and practicing safe sex. Cautionary rappers include: Kool Moe Dee, Gang Starr, MC Shan, Kid 'N Play, De La Soul.

Of all the genres known to modern music, gangsta rap surely has the corner on the most outrageous, most shocking lyrics. It's one thing to sing about alienation, rebellion, and disenchantment—which heavy metal and alternative groups also do; it's quite another to sing explicitly about sex acts, cop killing, and blowing people's brains out, which gangsta rap does all the time.

When to Worry

The number one question to ask when concerned about the music your teen listens to is: Is my teen progressing in the other areas of adolescent behavior—at home, in social relationships, at school? "If your kid is a good kid who's getting his work done at school and home, then no problem," says clinical psychologist Ruth Peters, Ph.D., of Clearwater, Florida, who specializes in child and adolescent psychology and media issues affecting young people. "Plenty of kids have their heads on straight but are very artistically inclined and into music. That's just their thing."

Do worry when your teen is having difficulty within the family, in school, or with friends and focuses a lot of time and energy on a disturbing type of music—plus the accessories and accessory thoughts that go with it, she says. "If your kid is into white supremacist music, that's probably a symptom of something going wrong in his life. It's not that the kid is a white supremacist but rather that he feels so bad about himself that he needs a quick fix to feel part of some group. The more he mouths the music, the more accepted he is within a group, perhaps for the first time in his life."

Changing physical appearance to conform to a musical type—be it wearing metal jewelry or leather, getting a tattoo, piercing a body part, or simply buying some T-shirts—is a quick way for a teen to buy access into a group. It's also a warning sign for parents that trouble might be brewing. "Kids need two things: balance—a healthy mix of home life, school, and friends—and focus—goals like college, technical school, or a job," Peters says. "I look at these musical cult–like things as a haven for kids who are out there wandering mentally. We're not talking about adolescent girls with crushes on teen idols and posters all over their rooms. They know that's fantasy. We're talking about a cultlike following of a particular music and the philosophy it espouses. You don't see kids with goals—kids on sports teams, for instance—getting into this stuff."

Don't worry if your kid gets home, does her homework, has dinner with the family, and then goes to her room to listen to music, Peters advises. "*Do* be concerned if your kid gets home in a snarly, surly mood, wants no communication with other family members, doesn't eat dinner with you, and withdraws into her room, the music, and like-minded friends. Sneak-

The Ugly

NWA
Ice Cube
Ice-T
Public Enemy
Dr. Dre
Snoop Doggy Dogg
Eazy E
Nas
Too Short
Scarface
Tupac Shakur
Wu-Tang Clan
Cypress Hill
Boss
Onyx
2-Live Crew
The Geto Boys
Luther Campbell
Schoolly D
. . . and many more

A Quick Pronunciation Guide

Dr. Dre = Dray, as in tray (*not* Dree)
Snoop Doggy Dog = Pronounced like it looks, but *never* Snoopy, please!
Monie Love = MOE-nee, not money
Tone Loc = It's Loke as in broke, in case you were wondering.
MC Lyte = M-C Lyte, NOT McLyte
Mary J. Blige = pronounce the "g" as in oblige
Jodeci = JOE-duh-see
En Vogue = N Vogue (not ON Vogue)
De La Soul = DAY-lah-soul (not Duh)

Ya got it? Cool.

ing out at night or sneaking friends into the house is another trouble sign."

What to Do

"If your kid is doing okay overall and you don't like the music, you might want to learn to live with it," says Peters. "But you also might say, 'We don't want your little sister or brother listening to this; you're going to have to use headphones.' Similarly, if their musical tastes are spilling over into their clothing tastes, don't be afraid to say, 'I don't want you to wear obscene clothing because that not only reflects on you, it reflects on our family.'" If it's infringing on your life, she notes, "you have the right to do that. It's your house."

If your teen listens to music you feel is bigoted, sexist, or otherwise objectionable, you might say, "You can listen to this, but only if you read this book or watch this movie with me," Peters advises. "For instance, if your son has been listening to white supremacist music and drawing swastikas on his notebook, you might suggest viewing the movie *Schindler's List* together and discussing it. Then, if they still want to do this—as long as they're doing well in other areas—it's okay. The kid who is really balanced is probably doing it for a lark and will come to his senses."

If your child brings home recordings you don't approve of, explain your objections and listen to her feelings about the music, suggests the Parents Music Resource Center in its materials for parents. If your child buys a record and then finds out it contains an objectionable song, offer to buy the record back or help your youngster return it to the store for a refund, the group suggests. This way you're not penalizing your child for being honest and trying to live by your family's standards.

Don't flat-out forbid teens to listen to certain types of music, Peters warns. They're just going to rebel. Appeal to their sense of reason through discussions of lyrics and their meaning, she advises. This approach is fair and works with many teens.

Do attend a couple of rock concerts yourself, advises the Parents Music Resource Center. This will help familiarize you with the scene, security in various venues, and seating plans (first-come first-served "festival" seating has led to deadly stampedes in the past; assigned concert seats are preferable). If you don't like what you find, complain to the management and community officials.

"If you have a problem kid, *don't* focus on the music. Focus on what is wrong with the kid's life and do something about it," Peters advises. "Parents need to take responsibility for what's going on in their kids' lives and not blame the music."

TV: GROWING UP IN THE GLOW

Teenagers spend a lot of time watching television—an average of 22 hours per week, by most estimates. Sixteen- to 17-year-olds, for instance,

THE SWITCHED-ON, TUNED-IN GENERATION

- **TV vs. homework: Twelve- to 17-year-olds watch an average of 3 hours of television a day.* Young people ages 14 to 15 spend an average of 1.6 hours on homework on school nights.****
- **TV/cable in their rooms: Of 14- to 15-year-olds who have their own rooms, 54 percent have their own TV; 36 percent have cable.****

Sources: *Nielsen Media Research
****Nickelodeon/Yankelovich Youth Monitor U.S., 1993 (a representative sample of 1,216 children ages 6 to 17)**

A Beginner's Guide to Beavis and Butt-head

- Beavis is the one with the reddish-blond hair. Butt-head has the brown hair and braces.
- Beavis and Butt-head attend Highland High School, where they sit together in the back of the class, often picking their noses (not each other's—their own).
- Typical exchange between Beavis and Butt-head:
  Beavis: "Heh heh m heh heh. Huh huh. Yeah."
  Butt-head: "Shut up."
- Some of Beavis and Butt-head's favorite words and phrases: Cool. Sucks (as in "school sucks," "life sucks," etc.). Nachos rule.

spend more time watching TV shows than doing homework, going to friends' houses, playing outside, or doing chores, according to the 1993 Nickelodeon/Yankelovich Youth Monitor U.S.

The range of programs available grows ever wider as cable and videocassette rentals increase the choices, but it's ABC, CBS, NBC, and FOX prime-time shows—youth-oriented programs especially—that remain the big favorites. MTV is up there, but not all teens have cable in the house. Those who do include MTV's *The Real World* (a documentary-style chronicle of real-life twentysomethings coping with life in the 90s) among their favorite shows, according to Irma Zandl, president of the Zandl Group, a teen-focused marketing consulting firm based in New York City. In 1994, Queen Latifah's sitcom, *Living Single*, and Fox's eerie *X-Files,* with its supernatural stories, became new teen TV favorites, the Zandl Group found. In case you were wondering, PBS and news programs do not attract teens in nearly the numbers many parents would like.

It's Tubular

Every network has its teen-appeal shows, and young people seem pretty tuned in to them all. Often teens are watching the same prime-time shows you are—*Roseanne, Home Improvement,* and *Married with Children* among them. No one has to tell you how popular *Beverly Hills 90210, Melrose Place, Martin,* and *Blossom* are with this age group. And from every show with a teenage character, teenage viewers ensure young stars are born—*Blossom*'s Mayim Bialik, for instance. While the name Joey Lawrence may not mean much to *you,* if you've got a teenage daughter in the house, his picture may well be plastered on her wall, his bio emblazoned in her memory. And then, of course, there's *Beavis and Butt-head.*

Bewildered Parents vs. *Beavis and Butt-head*

You find the show inane at best—offensive at the very least. Except for perhaps a very rare occasion, you fail to see the humor. Your kids find it a total crackup. They don't know what you're so upset about.

Despite raging controversy over the program's content and MTV's move of the show from 7 P.M. to a much later time slot, plenty of teens are still watching (or videotaping). *Beavis and Butt-head* is one of MTV's top-rated shows.

The more parents hate it, the more teens love it. "There is this intrinsic need to pick up on something parents despise," says Dr. Victor Strasburger, chief of adolescent medicine at the University of New Mexico at Albuquerque. "I always say if parents would listen to Dr. Dre and Metallica, our kids would start listening to Bach and Beethoven."

Dr. Strasburger sees *The Simpsons* as "a much healthier version of *Beavis and Butt-head.* It shows you can challenge the system, you can be provocative, you can amuse kids but still be socially responsible. *The Simpsons* is first-class television. *Beavis and Butt-head* is the pits."

Burn it. Dude. Chicks. Ass. Asswipe. Ozzy rules.

- **Beavis and Butt-head spend about a third of their show watching—and commenting on—music videos. Another third consists of their cartoon hijinks at school, around the house, around town. Another third (or so it seems, anyway) is commercials.**
- **Butt-head's philosophy of life as defined by Charles M. Young in *Rolling Stone*: "I like stuff that's cool" and "I don't like stuff that sucks." Beavis's philosophy of life: "I agree with Butt-head."**
- ***TV Guide* recently called Beavis and Butt-head "perhaps the truest representatives of teenage America in 1994."**

"A quiet evening at home presents an ordinary viewer with a cornucopia of political, criminal and psychopathological deviance. Some of the acts shown on television are so arcane that they were once familiar only to hardened big-city cops."

—Dr. Deborah Prothrow-Stith, *Deadly Consequences* (HarperCollins, 1991)

What to do if your teen watches *Beavis and Butt-head* and you don't approve: "If it's one of the battles you choose to fight," says Dr. Strasburger, "sit down with your children and watch the show together. Tell them, 'This is what I object to.' You may decide to ban it at home. At least let them know how you feel about it. Then, even if they run to a friend's house every day to watch it, they have to incorporate your views into their thinking." Dr. Strasburger adds, "Adults control the networks. Adults control rock music. Adults run MTV. Before we blame teens for their outrageous tastes, I think we have to look at what we as adults are setting up for them."

Deviance Rules

Woe is us. Beavis and Butt-head—like a lot of aspects of teenage culture parents wish would go away—are still here, getting huge ratings and now established as cultural icons of this generation of teens. And why not? The "crap" and "bitch" barriers have been long since broken on mainstream network TV. Sunday night, for instance, America's family night together, frequently finds prime time populated by a cavalcade of made-for-TV-movie deviants and their real-life stories, running the gamut from serial killings to familial sex crimes to schemes of bloody revenge. The talk shows in the after-school hours are peopled by transsexuals, strippers, children who killed their parents, and parents who killed their children. Should the evolution of two pyro-obsessed, music-crazed, insect-torturing, fart-focused young men *really* be such a surprise to anybody?

While you might call the parents of today's teens "the generation that TV built," plenty of those who have studied the ever more violent and sexually explicit TV fare would call this generation of teens "the generation that TV destroyed." "The level of violence on commercial television has remained constant during nearly two decades," concludes the 1993 *Report of the American Psychological Association Commission on Violence and Youth.* "Although there is less research on cable television and video," the report continues, "the rate of violence for MTV, for example, far exceeds that on commercial television."

Recent promises to clean up TV's act made by industry execs before U.S. congressional committees sound all too familiar and hold out only the hollowest of hopes. Testifying before the Senate Commerce Committee in late 1993, Howard Stringer, president of the CBS Broadcast Group, insisted, "There is less violence than ever before" on network TV and stated, "Voluntary self-regulation is working."

Psychologists worry most about TV and younger teens, since this age group arrives home after school to an empty house and, being too young to drive and too young to work, is left to watch MTV and talk shows while still an at impressionable age and with no adult around to advise or supervise.

In Your Face: TV Violence

The average American child has watched 8,000 murders and 100,000 acts of violence on television by the end of elementary school, according to a 1992 report by the American Psychological Association.

The Box

The Box is an increasingly popular "interactive" music television service reaching more than 18 million cable TV viewers in 1994, according to Miami-based Video Jukebox Network, which runs the service. The Box is now widely available. It's kind of like the old days, when you called your favorite radio station from a slumber party and asked the DJ to play a request, except in this case you're calling a local cable outlet and the request costs money—$1.99 for one video or three choices for $5.00. (The charges show up on your phone bill.) But that doesn't stop millions of teens from dialing the

MTV: A WINDOW ON TEEN CULTURE

MTV, a cultural pipeline for millions of American teenagers, is available to 58 million cable subscribers in this country. It remains the most widely watched music video service, offering such regular programs for its 12- to 34-year-old target audience as *Yo! MTV Raps* (rap music), *MTV Jams* (R&B, hip-hop, and some rap), *Alternative Nation* (just what it sounds like), *Headbangers Ball* (harder rock, metal, heavy metal), and *The Grind* (dance music). And then there are MTV's fashion, sports, and news (music industry news mostly) programs, specials, and documentaries.

Of all the sources of information for *parents* on teenage culture, MTV is among the most important, I found. Its music videos and shows—and, equally important, its commercials—are a significant reflection of the interests and pressures affecting teens today. If you don't watch MTV, you should do so occasionally. If you don't like what you see, discuss it with your teen, who may watch only enough to stay plugged in to the music scene. If you're concerned, there are several ways to "block" channels you don't like from coming into your home.

For all its popularity with some teens, MTV remains the scourge of a lot of parents, who find music video content violent, offensive, sexist, and suggestive of all kinds of aberrant behavior. Though MTV has been known to reject the most offensive hard-core videos, cleaned-up versions resubmitted by the record companies may be aired. Judging from the content of music videos the author watched ad nauseam (don't get me wrong, there are some *great* music videos being made), the standard for what's "hard core" and therefore unairable is surely way, way out there.

Parents might be interested to know that many teens I encountered either didn't get MTV in their homes or were too busy with after-school sports and clubs, academic pursuits, or jobs to watch it much.

VIDEO GAMES: "BETTER THAN SLEEP, BETTER THAN SUPPER, AND A HECK OF A LOT BETTER THAN SCHOOL"

Ever since Atari came out with its electronic ping-pong game, Pong, in 1972, ever since the now seemingly primitive Pac-man invaded millions of American homes, video games have been part of the scene for teens and a great many adults. Today, according to a 1993 *Time* magazine article, Americans spend $5 billion a year on video games—$400 million more than they spend at the movies.

The constantly changing world of video games presents new levels of involvement and reality for players—and concern for some parents. With Hollywood, Silicon Valley, and video game producers all hard at work cre-

900 number, punching in the three-digit code for the video they want to see, and waiting the 20 minutes or less it takes for their video request to show up on their home screen.

Teens really adore the Box. They say it better reflects the musical tastes of the moment because it's driven by the tastes of other music fans in their area as opposed to programmed choices by national music networks, where music industry politics and promotion pressures may more likely come into play.

Teens also say they like having the power to program their own choices.

Two Views on Video Games

"It's worse than TV or a movie. It communicates the message that the only way to be empowered is through violence."
—Prof. Marsha Kinder, University of Southern California, in *Time* magazine, 1993

"You had a bad day so you can go in there and rip a couple of heads off and feel better."
—unidentified video-store manager, in *Time* magazine, 1993

ating ever more dazzling, colorful, complex, lifelike software—and the hardware to run it—the possibilities for what may very soon come together in your living room and in cyberspace are, quite literally, exploding.

Today's games and newer, more technically powerful playing gear like 3DO, Atari's Jaguar, and other 64-bit systems allow youngsters to enter an extraordinary range of worlds—from those of favorite cartoons, Hollywood movies, and sports stars to frightening fantasy lands and violent urban settings. Now (Sonic the Hedgehog, Super Mario Brothers, and NBA Jam notwithstanding), you see the blood, you experience tension, and in some games you literally point the gun at your TV screen, assume a firing stance, and blast away at the bad guys. (A plastic, life-size revolver used in just that way comes with the home game "Lethal Enforcer," for instance.) The better to improve their eye-hand coordination, teens say, as they lop off heads, rip out hearts, and go on their merry way.

Who's Playing? And How Much?

While primarily still the province of 8- to 15-year-old boys, video games hold a major attraction (sometimes one of obsessional proportions) for older teenage males and some adults. An estimated 50 million American homes have either Sega or Nintendo systems, and among teens with video games at home, average playing time is approximately 1.5 hours a day. Additionally, there is the seemingly infinite world of "expert knowledge" on the games—books, magazines, and toll-free info lines offering playing tips, strategies, and incredibly detailed histories of game characters.

So Real It's Unreal

As virtual reality and interactive television become commonplace"young people will become even more deeply immersed in the games they play, using their entire bodies and not just their eyes and hands to decide the direction in which a game will go," explains Eugene Provenzo Jr., Ph.D., professor of education at the University of Miami and an expert on today's video games and their impact on young people. The very near future (and the present in some of the glitzier video arcades), incorporates data gloves, projection helmets, and "surround around" goggles (or "eyephones," as they're sometimes called) with which you enter simulated worlds where you participate using your whole body. "It represents the beginning of a whole new phase of video game technology," Provenzo says, "one that is potentially wonderful and potentially frightening."

What's the Fuss?

Proponents of video games and young players I spoke with say there's little difference between video games and those played with toy soldiers or plastic cowboys and Indians—imaginary fighting games that for generations have also featured shoot 'em up play that left combatants dead or wounded, albeit scattered around the living room floor. They see today's

The 1993 furor over the more-gruesome-than-usual violence in "Mortal Kombat" propelled its sales into the stratosphere. Its sequel, not surprisingly, is an even bloodier "Mortal Kombat II." Controversy over "Night Trap"—wherein female victims who have had their blood sucked from their necks are later hanged from meat hooks—took a relatively unnoticed game and turned it into a hot seller.

Just how many teenagers use computers, anyway? Nearly 70 percent of teens ages 14 to 17 reported using a computer in school at least once a week, according to the Nickelodeon/ Yankelovich Youth Monitor U.S. 1993. That's up from 41 percent in 1988.

games as no worse, say, than a Kung Fu movie or a 1970s-style game of pre-computerized Dungeons and Dragons.

Some Advice for Worried Parents

While we wait for the technology that will soon enable every teen to merge video games with home computers and fiber-optic connections to the world, parents still need to be concerned about the content of some of the games kids play.

Though Nintendo says it polices itself (its version of the 1993 bloody blockbuster hit "Mortal Kombat" was somewhat more sanitized than Sega's), its standards for what's too graphic or too violent may not be yours. Sega offers ratings guidelines on its game boxes—its own voluntary classifications, don't forget—and experts remind parents that sometimes an MA-17 rating (mature audiences, 17 and older) does more to increase than deter purchases. Also, there's no law that says you can't sell an MA-17 game to a 14-year-old.

Violence is still something parents need to be watching out for, notes Eugene Provenzo, who is also author of the book *Video Kids* (Harvard University Press, 1991). "Parents need to be aware of the potential for their kids to imitate what they see on the screen," he explains. "There is also sexism in the games. Parents should know how women are depicted, since the idea of women as victims predominates. They should also be concerned about racism, which shows up too—such as Asian-American bashing and even homophobia."

Even teens themselves think some of today's video games are over the top. Some teen aficionados I talked with were quick to suggest games they felt parents should become acquainted with if they find them on their own teen's shelf. Among video games they cite "Mortal Kombat" and "Streetfighter." Among computer games they mention "Metal and Lace: Battle of the Robobabes" and "Doom," which one teenager, a self-confessed former video game addict, described as "one of the most horrific. Definitely the bloodiest out there." While these teens do *not* believe such games should be censored, they *do* think greater parental interest is needed.

"At $60 or $70 or $80 a pop, parents are usually paying for it," one 16-year-old video game junkie added. "They should know what their kids are getting."

How Much is Too Much?

"If the kid comes home and wants to play for half an hour or an hour each day, that's not a big problem," Provenzo says. "But when kids are playing two and a half, three, or four hours a day, you've got trouble." He also reminds parents that the first night or two a teenager has a new game, playing time may be longer than usual, but that's okay.

Families with children under 18 are more likely than any other group to have computers at home—26 percent of them had personal computers in the house in 1992, according to a report in *American Demographics* magazine. While the number of teens with the hardware and software to access cyberspace at home is still relatively small, it's a fast-growing field, and young people are able to enter it with comfort and ease.

Jason Goldman, a 17-year-old Midwestern high school student who works in a computer store after school and on weekends, says he has encountered kiddie porn and other hard-core conversation and games—among other things—on various bulletin boards when online on his home computer. "If you get into this too much, as some kids do, it can be really weird," he says.

In general, "it's a case of let the buyer—or renter—beware," Provenzo adds. "Review the games. Play them yourself. If there's a problem, discuss it with your child. A lot of people say, 'I don't have time to do that.' But if you've got kids, you've got the responsibility."

CYBERSPACE 101: AN INTRODUCTORY COURSE

Cyberschools. Cybershopping. Cybertunes. Cybersex. Welcome to cyberspace, the information superhighway where most assuredly a teenager—perhaps your own—will be your guide. While it most likely boggles your mind, *they're* totally plugged in, poised to pounce on the next wrinkle in the rapidly advancing technology.

A Brave New World

In cyberspace, the possibilities are already mind-boggling—access to enormous libraries of information, data banks, news and sports information services, newspaper and magazine libraries, financial markets, forums of all kinds, systems, software, shopping services—all of it quick and easily available to anyone with the right equipment, a modem, and half a cyberbrain.

From the comfort of their own home, teens can now dial into billboards to meet like-minded teens on CompuServe, America Online, and Prodigy (all of which have mechanisms—though not foolproof ones—for policing their networks to minimize offensive behavior and keep adults out of cyberturf designed strictly for teens and younger kids), but, more significantly, they can access literally thousands of little local bulletin boards where anything (and anyone) goes.

Where Worlds Collide

On the network of networks, the Internet, some 20 million people and thousands of educational institutions, government offices, and businesses in dozens of countries can interconnect at any hour of the day or night. In cyberspace, a global conclave of dazzlingly brilliant, cutting-edge thinkers is possible at any moment.

The bad news is that through computer-linked bulletin boards and adult-oriented sex forums teens may also exchange information and have e-mail experiences that might shock their parents—sharing sexual fantasies and pairing up with electronic partners whose identities and influence may be the stuff of parents' worst nightmares. Teens (and adults for that matter) can spend long hours delving deep into the computer netherworld. And the anonymity of the computer screen leaves open the possibility of creating a cyberspace identity—or "cyberego"—that bears little resemblance to a person's real-life identity.

A teen's partner in a cyberspace video game can be another youngster or an adult half a world away. Whole libraries of games can be accessed as part of your basic monthly service. You'll find, for example, "virtual amusement parks" like the ImagiNation Network, described by *Time* magazine in 1993 as "a combination of Las Vegas, Nintendo, and Sunday-afternoon social club." Here, fellow computer users can compete in everything from medieval role-playing fantasies to games of bridge and blackjack.

On the Learning Network (a 23-nation social studies and literature program run by AT&T) or on the National Geographic Kids Network (linking more than 10,000 elementary school classes in science experiments), students who might otherwise be turned off to learning plug in and turn on. Teachers—and teens—in schools that have such capabilities have high praise for the technology.

Learning in Cyberspace

The good news is that computernets being used in the classroom enable children to learn and work in astonishing new ways, improving their math, geography, science, and reasoning skills and positioning them for excellent jobs in the future.

The Cost of Computing

For school districts and parents, teen travel on the information superhighway doesn't always come cheap. The hardware and software can be expensive. And then you get a monthly bill—$8.95 a month (as of 1994) for CompuServe basic services, for instance—plus extra charges once you exceed basic use minimums.

This is one more area where parents of teens need to be involved and vigilant—to act, if you will, as the information superhighway patrol.

Advice for Parents of Cyberspace Travelers

"As with any place you allow your children to go, you have to set out rules for them" when they begin exploring cyberspace, says Jake Winebaum, editor in chief of *Family PC* magazine. "Just as you would tell them not to give out information such as name, phone number, or home address to strangers on the street, the same goes for cyberspace. Instruct them not to give out personal information and *never* to meet [in person] *anyone* they have met online without first getting your permission."

Adds Winebaum, "The other thing parents can and should do is get involved. Sit down with your kids at their computers and learn the services with them—or better yet, let them teach you! Young people who see their parents are really interested and involved are more likely to be responsible users of today's fantastic computer services."

"The world of online computer services is like a mall where there are all kinds of crazy stores as well as normal ones," says Jake Winebaum of *Family PC* magazine. "Kids hang out there and, without a parent monitoring, can wander wherever they want to, alone."

Smart Teens/ Foolish Choices

Trouble and teens seem to go hand in hand. Drugs, alcohol, guns, gangs—in the 90s, these are just some of the everyday dangers of teen life. The risks are no longer limited to big cities; kids everywhere are faced with the pressures and stresses that lead to substance abuse, even suicide. And the threat of violence lurks everywhere. For many kids, drinking, drug use, and other dangerous behaviors may just be part of a fleeting phase, but for others they can lead to long-term problems—or worse. What can a parent do? Be alert, be aware, be ready to listen and to help when you can—and know when it's time to turn to professionals.

Teens Speak on Drug Use

"Drugs are so mainstream now. It's simply cool to do it. Teachers aren't aware of the problem. The well-off kids are into it now, the ones who looked down on others who did it."
—Trisha,* 16, Columbus, Ohio

"I have never seen drugs except on TV. Where I live it's not a hip thing. It's not something you would talk about doing."
—Autumn Michelle Bobo, 17, Calhoun County, Alabama

"Legalizing pot is a *major* issue with kids today."
—Aaron Shin, 18, Tucson

TEENAGE DRUG ABUSE: A QUESTION OF STYLE AND SUBSTANCES

"Just Say No," the watchwords of the 1980s, seem to be making way for a "Just Say Maybe" attitude among teenagers now.

"Certainly the combination of drugs now growing in popularity—marijuana, LSD, and amphetamines—is reminiscent of what was popular in the early days of the drug epidemic," said Lloyd Johnston, Ph.D., program director of the University of Michigan's Institute for Social Research Monitoring the Future Study, early in 1994. "Other drugs then followed in popularity. I certainly hope that we are not seeing a rebirth of the old epidemic." The Monitoring the Future Study, funded by the National Institute on Drug Abuse, is considered the most reliable source of information on drug use among adolescents. Its latest findings made teenage drug use—for the first time in a long time—front-page news.

Looking at teenage culture and the re-emergence of drug symbolism—marijuana in particular—there is no mistaking it: The drug culture, demonized for a decade, is staging a strong return.

It's in the Numbers

During the 1980s and into the 1990s, teenage drug use dropped sharply—from 66 percent of seniors reporting at least one-time use of illicit drugs in 1981 to 41 percent of seniors saying the same in 1992, according to data from the University of Michigan study.

But in 1992, experts raised worried eyebrows when an increase in drug use among young teens was observed, and 1993 figures dashed any hopes that those upticks might be just an aberration.

Pot is Hot

Leaves. Cloves. Blunts. Bud. Herb. Chronic. Stash. These are among many current terms for marijuana. The names change—and so has the substance. Some parents may hold fond memories of pot as a harmless high, just part of the fun, along with good music, good friends, and lots of greasy, sugary foods consumed in great quantities. But drug abuse experts warn that the pot of today is a whole lot stronger—perhaps as much as 20 times more potent—and a "gateway" to other kinds of substance abuse. Kids, however, still see it as a "safe" high. "Compared to other kinds of drugs, pot is natural. It grows in the ground," says Monica, a high school junior in northern California's Mendocino County. That's not an uncommon view among teens today.

Back in Fashion

"Pot fashion, not long ago the province of losers or outcasts, has suddenly become hip, blossoming into a $10 million to $15 million business," noted *Newsweek* in late 1993.

A Celebration in Song

Celebrating marijuana in song is now fashionable (and profitable). Though not alone in the pro-pot musical vanguard, the rap group Cypress Hill is perhaps the best-known band riding a wave of success with songs like "Hits from the Bong," and "Legalize It." (Maybe you've seen their pot-inspired clothing line, with sales upwards of $6 million last year.) Rapper Dr. Dre's album *The Chronic* was a mega-seller named for a very strong type of marijuana. A giant marijuana leaf served as the backdrop for the Black Crowes on a recent tour.

In Your Face: Teen Drug Use

Marijuana use by high school seniors was on the decline for 14 years—but no more. When the University of Michigan studied approximately 50,000 students nationwide in more than 400 junior and senior high schools, 26 percent of 1993 seniors reported using marijuana at least once in the past year, up from 22 percent in 1992. Among tenth graders, 19 percent had used marijuana once or more in the previous year, up from 15 percent in 1992. Eighth graders, too, showed a marked increase in annual marijuana use—up to 9 percent in 1993 from 7 percent in 1992.

And so it is. You'll find the multipointed leaf emblazoned on everything from sweatshirts to silver medallions and worn on everyone from the most innocent suburban teen to youthful drug dealers. "*Everybody* wears the marijuana symbol on hats, earrings, something—even people who don't smoke themselves," says 18-year-old Aaron Shin of Tucson.

"My younger brother, who's a freshman, wears a jacket with a big marijuana leaf on the back," says a junior at suburban Chicago's New Trier High School. "I don't think it means anything special to him. It's just something a lot of kids do."

Not Just Pot

LSD is back in a big way too. Teens now are doing "drop" (as some call acid now) at rates just below the 7.2 percent peak in 1975, when the Monitoring the Future Study began. Even scarier, indications are that heroin is making a quiet comeback among twentysomethings, who often set the tone for the younger set. Today, smoking or snorting heroin is preferred over injection.

One drug of the moment is GHB—gamma-hydroxy-butyrate—a potentially deadly synthetic steroid usually dissolved in water, sometimes laced with Valium. Oft sold in big-city dance clubs, oft seen in L.A. nightclubs, and a fave at raves, GHB is sold in liquid form in small crack vial–like canisters and has developed a reputation for producing euphoric effects. Last year, rock star Billy Idol came close to adding his name to the list of drug-done-in performers, nearly overdosing when he collapsed in convulsions outside a Hollywood club after reportedly taking GHB. Other substances on the scene include Ecstasy—still a big-time feel-good drug—as well as nitrous oxide balloons, Special K (as some call the hallucinogen Ketamine), and many fearsome more.

Back to the Future

Rock musicians—ever the teenage heroes—were drug proponents in the 1960s and 1970s but in the 1980s shifted to vilifying, not glorifying, drug use. Amid supportive cheers, rock stars with varying substance abuse problems proclaimed themselves "clean," crediting 12-step programs embraced by the rich, famous, and dependent-no-more.

But that trend seems to have halted. This generation of teens need not look nearly so far back as Jimi Hendrix or Janis Joplin for drug casualties among its music heroes. Major music stars like Nirvana's late lead singer, Kurt Cobain, and his wife, Courtney Love, had admitted to using heroin long before Cobain's drug-and-alcohol-induced coma, which preceded his April 1994 suicide by just a few weeks. Cobain's long-standing emotional turmoil combined with his history of substance abuse were critical factors in his death. And then there's Hollywood: In late 1993, 23-year-old actor River Phoenix dropped dead from a cocaine and heroin overdose outside the Viper Club, a popular L.A. nightspot, blowing the lid off a reported new surge of illicit drug use among Hollywood's privileged younger set.

In 1993 teenage LSD use also reached its highest level in years—18 years, to be exact—with 6.8 percent of seniors reporting they had used LSD at least once during the previous year.

Movies and TV Getting in on the Act

Dazed and Confused, **the 1993 movie from director Richard Linklater (director of the popular Generation X film *Slacker*), showed teenage moviegoers life as lived in a marijuana haze by a group of high school kids in 1976. Even more teens, no doubt, saw the episode of TV's *Roseanne* in which the show's principal characters discover a ten-year-old stash, try it out, and giggle their way to the closing credits.**

THE HIGH THAT CAN PUT YOU SIX FEET UNDER

Teens call it "huffing" or "spooky" and say "I'm huffed up" or "spooked out." Depending on where you live, there may be any number of other terms for it. But whatever you call it, inhaling chemical vapors from everyday household products is a common and sometimes deadly activity. It is most popular among 13- to 14-year-olds.

When one kid calls another kid a "spray head," it's not about hairstyles. It's about household products that are right under your nose—and, perhaps, under your kid's nose too. In 1993, 19 percent of eighth graders reported that they had used inhalants at least once, according to the Monitoring the Future Study conducted by the University of Michigan's Institute for Social Research. That figure was up from 17 percent just one year earlier.

We're talkin' stuff that's in your cupboard, your bathroom, your garage. Whipped cream and vegetable spray dispensers (teens inhale the propellant gases used in aerosol cans). Marking pens. Nail polish remover. Typewriter correction fluid. Gasoline. Propane. Butane from disposable lighters. Spray paint (gold, silver, and clear are the most abused). Paint thinner. Nitrous oxide (potentially deadly and sometimes sold at rock concerts in balloons for inhalation; not to be confused with helium, which does not produce euphoric effects). Halon gas in fire extinguishers. And among the most deadly of all (despite a clear warning on the can from the manufacturer), Scotchguard.

Dangerous, Sometimes Deadly

According to inhalant abuse experts, sniffing volatile substances can cause severe damage to the brain and can damage the central nervous system as well. Some of the chemicals kids abuse can starve the body of oxygen, causing the heart to beat faster and more erratically, resulting in death among the young adolescents who are the biggest users.

"Kids use these substances to get a buzz, a buzz that can last from 30 seconds to 20 minutes or longer, depending on how long they continue to sniff," explains Theresa Jacobsen, an inhalant abuse counselor and executive director of the Colorado Inhalant Abuse Program in Denver. "They can be inhaled by mouth—which some teens call 'huffing'—by nose, or both."

No Teenager Is Immune

"Inhalants are an equal-opportunity substance," says Harvey Weiss, project director for the Texas Prevention Partnership in Austin and chairperson of the National Inhalant Prevention Coalition. Weiss believes it's important to dispel the notion that this is a ghetto or barrio problem. It is just as common in the suburbs and rural areas.

"We call this the silent epidemic because of the depth and breadth of usage that people just don't talk about," Weiss says. "There are documented cases of sudden sniffing deaths where first-time usage could be

While parents worry about teens using crack cocaine, LSD, or heroin, on the list of substances most abused by teens, *inhalants* rank just behind marijuana (number three), cigarettes (number two), and alcohol (number one by far), the University of Michigan's Monitoring the Future Study found.

"Inhalants are probably the most dangerous thing [kids] could be involved in," says a Denver-area mother taken completely by surprise when her 14-year-old daughter was caught by police using inhalants in a local park. "As a parent, it was devastating. Afterwards, she told me she was no longer doing it, and we kept a close eye on her. But I had a funny feeling, so I searched her room and found the stuff—spray paint you can get in Kmart. And you're *supposed* to be 18 to buy these."

last-time usage. This is why you read about perfectly nice youngsters from good families dying this way."

Sudden sniffing death and addiction (yes, kids do become addicted) aren't the only hazards. Kids sometimes get so high they cross a highway and get killed by oncoming traffic, Jacobsen reports. Or teens huffing gasoline may light up a cigarette and suffer fatal burns.

Most teenagers at some time in their lives are confronted with the choice to try, or not try, inhalants. "All these inhalants are poisons," Jacobsen notes. "You don't put pesticides in your body. Why would you do solvents?"

Good question. It's one you just might want to discuss with your kid.

PUMPING TROUBLE: ANABOLIC STEROIDS

It is one of the most secret sides of teenage culture today—practiced very privately by a relative handful of teenagers, guys mostly, but very frightening to substance abuse experts, physicians, and coaches familiar with its effects. Kids call it "juicing" or "roiding." By any name, using anabolic steroids is a dangerous game teens are playing with their health.

Though government-funded drug abuse studies show only tiny percentages of teens using these substances, Neil Carolin, a Syracuse, New York, specialist in the treatment of anabolic steroid abusers, believes as many as one million young people under age 18 may be using them.

"About 40 percent start using at age 15 or younger," he finds. The steroid user Carolin sees quite often is a younger teenage boy who looks in the mirror or at other guys in the shower room at school and thinks, 'I'm never going to attract girls this way.' Adds Carolin, "We're now seeing about a 60/40 split, nonathlete to athlete user. And it's not an inner-city drug. It's mostly suburban kids who use it."

Anabolic steroid abuse has been linked to kidney and liver damage, heart disease, shrunken testicles, mood swings, and stunted growth in adolescents. "The majority of steroids being used now are veterinary; they were meant for beef cattle, horses," Carolin explains. "One of the most common is called Winstrol-V. Kids call it 'winnie' or 'w.' The label reads loud and clear: 'Potent anabolic therapy for dogs, cats, and horses,' and somewhere in the information in the product packaging is a warning: 'Do not use in horses for food consumption,' " he says. "This is what kids are injecting. Among users, this is a very popular drug. The still-classic drug for first use is called Deca-Durabolin, or 'deca' on the street. Equipose is another popular—and veterinary—one."

It is not unusual for a steroid habit to cost $800 or $900 a month, Carolin says, "even double or triple that for big-time users." Withdrawal can be a long process.

Clues to teenage steroid abuse include: (1) an obsession with working out at the gym (not at the "Y" but at an "iron factory") and (2) an obses-

Scotchguard is the substance that scares inhalant abuse counselor Theresa Jacobsen most. When inhaled, Scotchguard does to the lungs just what it is designed to do to fabric: keeps fluid from being able to permeate it. "What it does is coat the lungs, and what happens is the individual drowns in his own fluids because fluids are trapped in the lungs," she says. Not a pretty picture.

Steroids, while illegal, are still easy enough to obtain, usually from other kids. Since oral steroids are slow to be absorbed, the switch to injections is fairly rapid. For a young male desperate to put on some muscle and gain some size, the fear of needles is quickly overcome.

Within a couple of months, the steroids have worked and the teenager is on his way to becoming a hulk, and hooked—if not physically, at least psychologically—on the body-expanding drugs.

sion with nutrition. "It's abnormal for a kid at 13 or 14 or 15 to be preoccupied with diet, calories, fat content, and working out at the gym," says Carolin. Tiny blood stains on a teen's underwear—remnants of an injection—are something else parents might notice.

"I've had parents bring in a whole shoe box full of steroids and syringes and ask, 'What's this?' " relates Carolin. "And when I tell them 'anabolic steroids,' they say, 'Thank God! I thought it was one of those serious drugs.' " Anabolic steroids, folks, *are* serious drugs.

SMOKING

Cigarette smoking remains a popular teenage activity—and a hotly debated issue among students in many schools (especially, teens say, when teachers are permitted to puff away in staff lounges). The daily smoking rate for high school seniors dropped considerably between 1977 and 1981 and remained steady until last year, but a major national study in 1993 found smoking among teens of all ages was on the rise again.

In the three decades since the surgeon general's first warnings on smoking and health, *adult* smoking has dropped dramatically, but "we've made a lot less progress with our young people—especially white females," according to U.S. Surgeon General Dr. Joycelyn Elders, whose Surgeon General's Report in 1994 pointedly noted the contrast between the number of adults quitting and the number of teens taking up the tobacco habit.

Why Teens Smoke

"Young people still smoke because they think it's cool," says Dr. Joseph DiFranza, associate professor of family and community medicine at the University of Massachusetts Medical Center, adding, "Teenagers are more likely to be regular smokers if their parents smoke."

Many teenage girls say they smoke to help control their weight. "I think this is the primary reason girls smoke more than boys now," Dr. DiFranza says, noting that the health risks of smoking far outweigh the poundage smoking may—or may not—help a teen keep off. Studies also show teens are more likely to smoke if they have no academic plans beyond high school and, as Dr. Elders noted, if they are white.

Black students seem more alert to the warnings about smoking. According to the University of Michigan's Monitoring the Future Study, funded by the National Institute on Drug Abuse, "black students have a much lower prevalence of daily smoking than white students (4 percent vs. 21 percent in their senior year); their smoking rate continued to decline after 1983, while the rate for whites stabilized."

An Image Thing

The cigarette has long been a part of the teenage scene in American high schools and middle schools. Its image has gone from 50s bad-kid

In Your Face: Teen Smoking

- **Almost half of all eighth graders say they have tried cigarettes.**
- **Half of eighth grade students do not think a pack-a-day smoker runs a great risk of harm from that behavior.**
- **28 percent of high school seniors are current cigarette smokers.**
- **53 percent of half-a-pack-a-day (or more) smokers in their senior year said they had tried to quit smoking but found they could not.**
- **Only 5 percent of daily smokers in high school in the mid-1980s thought they would "definitely" be smok-**

ing five years later. In follow-up studies seven to nine years later, nearly 75 percent of them were still smoking daily.

- **Initiation of daily smoking most often occurs in grades six through nine.**

Source: Monitoring the Future Study, 1993, University of Michigan Institute for Social Research

"Often we hear parents say, 'I caught my kids smoking cigarettes, but at least they're not doing drugs.' That's a terrible attitude because tobacco and nicotine kill more people than any other drug. It's also more difficult to break an addiction to nicotine than it is to stop smoking marijuana."

—Dr. Joseph DiFranza, associate professor of family and community medicine, University of Massachusetts Medical Center

cool to 70s health-conscious uncool to 80s high school political hot potato and back again. As sociologist and author Donna Gaines notes in her book *Teenage Wasteland: Suburbia's Dead End Kids* (HarperPerennial, 1991), what was once the symbol of juvenile delinquency in boys and trampiness in girls is again "the mark of the uncooperative teen, the rebel, the troublemaker." For teens who like the rebel label—and some do—cigarettes are just an accessory, a part of the image.

The Bottom Line

Public health officials, physicians, parents, and many nonsmoking teenagers remain alarmed about the current teenage smoking rates, and with good reason: Studies show that most teen smokers (including light smokers) believe they'll be able to stop smoking but end up as heavy smokers in their adult years. Also, many *younger* teens say they see no health risk from cigarettes. For these and other compelling reasons, smoking is still a critical teenage health concern.

TEENS AND DRINKING

While some teens may have turned in their "Party 'till You Puke" T-shirts for something with a "Party Smart" message, and while Students Against Driving Drunk (SADD) chapters and Safe Rides programs abound, drinking remains an extremely significant factor in the life and culture of teenagers in the 1990s. Many is the country dirt road on a warm summer night that leads to a bonfire, a keg, and a crowd of teenagers getting smashed.

"Drinking isn't any big deal. Everybody does it," says a high school junior from outside Baton Rouge. "Alcohol is beyond accepted. Parties aren't any good if it's not there," adds an Ohio teen.

Never mind that drinking's illegal for virtually all high school students. (The minimum drinking age is 21 in all 50 states and the District of Columbia.) Nearly 90 percent of high school seniors and nearly two-thirds of eighth graders say they have tried alcohol. So found the largest and most respected study of teenage substance abuse in the nation, the University of Michigan's Monitoring the Future Study, in its 1993 survey. Just over half of high school seniors (51 percent) and 42 percent of juniors surveyed said they had consumed alcohol in the previous 30-day period.

Binge Drinking

Binge drinking—consuming five or more alcoholic drinks in a row—is common practice among today's teens and a major concern for public health officials. In 1993, fully 28 percent of high school seniors and 23 percent of sophomores told researchers for the Monitoring the Future Study they had consumed five or more alcoholic beverages in a row in the prior two weeks. That's a lot of very drunk teens, a lot of the time.

Teens Speak on Drinking

"I'm seeing some of my friends who all they can think about is getting plastered on the weekend. It's what gets them through the week. They just can't wait for Friday night. It's kind of scary."

—Sarah Simmons, high school senior (class of '95), Columbia, South Carolina

"There are two main reasons kids [in my school] drink. One is to impress everybody—'Oh, I'm cool, I act grown up.' The other is to get away from some of their problems. And you think to yourself, 'How stupid. Do you need friends so bad you have to show off by drinking?' "

—David Reina, high school freshman (class of '98), Pearl River, New York

In Your Face: Teen Drinking

Percentage of teens who said they had consumed five or more alcoholic drinks in a row at least once during the prior two-week period in 1993:

Eighth graders	**14%**
Tenth graders	**23%**
Twelfth graders	**28%**

Source: Monitoring the Future Study, 1993, University of Michigan Institute for Social Research

Despite headway in getting through to teens with messages about the hazards of alcohol, too many still die under its influence—behind the wheel, in a car a drunken friend is driving, or in other kinds of accidents caused by impaired judgment. And later in life, many others become casualties of alcoholism begun in their youthful years. Then there's the well-documented link between drinking, violence, vandalism, and academic failure.

Why They Start

Why do young people start drinking? For its 1991 Roper Youth Report, Roper pollsters asked teenagers between 13 and 17 which people or things most influenced whether they drank alcohol. While many parents may believe pressure from peers is the biggest factor in a teen's decision to drink, the overwhelming influence cited by students was their *parents'* attitudes and actions (55 percent). The influence of best friends was cited by 24 percent. Only 4 percent said siblings were an influencing factor.

What about TV and advertising? Just 4 percent of teens surveyed said what they saw on television was an influence on drinking, and only 3 percent said what they see in ads affected their decision to drink or not to drink.

Though the last decade's campaign to educate teens about the risks of alcohol has succeeded in cutting teenage drinking substantially, plenty of adolescents are still drinking—early and often.

DIET RIOT

Potato chips. French fries. Pizza. Cookies. Donuts. Ice cream. Teenagers (girls especially) spend a lot of time thinking about these things. Or worrying about them. Or trying to avoid them. Or eating them and then throwing up. In a nation obsessed with weight and appearance, dieting is a prominent feature—and sometimes a serious problem—in the lives of many teens (and even younger boys and girls). Two leading eating disorders, anorexia nervosa (significant loss of original body weight through extreme dieting or exercise, accompanied by a disturbed body image) and bulimia nervosa (binging and purging, generally by self-induced vomiting), are illnesses of considerable concern for young people today.

"Unfortunately, girls are still growing up in an environment where the waif look remains idealized," says Dr. Michael Pertschuck, clinical associate professor of psychiatry at the University of Pennsylvania Medical Center in Philadelphia and a specialist in the psychological significance of appearance. "This is why you have girls even in fourth and fifth grade dieting. It's not unusual."

While many middle school and high school kids worry about their weight, medical experts say most teens don't understand the damage nutritional deprivation can cause—including vitamin and mineral

Though figures from the President's Council on Physical Fitness show that 20 percent of children between ages 6 and 17 are overweight, "studies show that 80 to 90 percent of tenth and eleventh grade girls diet because they *think* they're too fat," says Jane Rubel, president of ANRED, Anorexia Nervosa and Related Eating Disorders. "Fifty percent of fourth grade girls diet for the same reason," she adds.

Anorexia nervosa and bulimia nervosa occur in an estimated 1 in 100 young women—not an alarmingly large number, but studies show that 20 percent of teenage girls display at least one symptom of an eating disorder. And anorexia and bulimia can be extremely harmful, even deadly. Starvation results in death for approximately 5 percent of anorexics. Incidence of these illnesses in young males is far less common.

deficiencies, altered growth, and serious long-term effects such as a greater likelihood of weight gain and obesity in adulthood.

"In their early teens, boys are naturally building more muscle, so putting on weight doesn't go against what their bodies are doing," Dr. Pertschuck explains. "But a 13- or 14-year-old girl who looks at the curves that are developing and wants to diet is fighting her body, not going along with it."

Dieting to Excess

"An anorexic is someone with an overwhelming fear of being fat even when that person is of normal weight or thin," explains Jane Rubel, president of ANRED, Anorexia Nervosa and Related Eating Disorders, a national support and information organization in Eugene, Oregon. "Anorexics are never satisfied with the amount of weight they have lost; it always has to be more. Other signs include refusal to eat normal amounts of food, especially refusal to eat in front of other people, and wearing baggy clothes as a way to escape detection." Bulimics, on the other hand, are typically of normal weight and are thus more difficult to detect, medical experts say. "One of the prime giveaways in the case of a bulimic," Rubel adds, "is when someone eats and then, time and again, excuses herself and goes to the bathroom."

While "eat, drink, and be merry" remains the motto for millions of Dorito-gobbling, milk shake–guzzling teens, "eat, drink, and be wary" attitudes adopted by some teens *can* cross the line from healthy to hazardous.

SUICIDE AND DEPRESSION

When Nirvana lead singer Kurt Cobain put a shotgun to his head and pulled the trigger one chilly April night in Seattle earlier this year, the young man whose music, style, and persona figured prominently in the hearts and minds of millions of American teenagers took a step a great many young people ponder today, a step too many also take.

"Suicide is now hip, dangerous, the final resistance to adult authority, a last stand against authority," observes Donna Gaines in *Teenage Wasteland: Suburbia's Dead End Kids*. "To some kids, suicide is death before dishonor, heroism over defeat. Because attempts so greatly outnumber actual suicides, suicide is as much a statement of the desire to control life as to end it."

Even for teens who never consider suicide, the subject can often hit close to home—and a lot closer than the suicide of a music performer they admire. And in a recent Gallup Youth Survey, 60 percent of teens said they knew someone who either tried and failed to commit suicide or tried and succeeded. In approximately one of every three of those cases, the

In Your Face: Teen Suicide

- **Suicide is the second leading cause of death, after accidents, among white adolescents and young adults ages 15 to 24.**
- **The teenage suicide rate has tripled since the 1950s.**
- **An estimated 5,000 young people ages 15 to 24 kill themselves each year.**

Source: U.S. Dept of Health and Human Services

About 400,000 teenagers try to kill themselves each year, according to figures in the American Academy of Pediatrics book *Caring for Your Adolescent*, edited by Donald E. Greydanus, M.D. (Bantam, 1991).

depressed teen was either a close friend or a relative, the survey found. Six percent of teens told the Gallup pollsters they had attempted suicide themselves. Fifteen percent said they had come close to attempting it.

A Frequent Theme in Contemporary Teen Media

Most likely, if the parents of today's teens thought about suicide at all during their teen years, it was in English class, reading Shakespeare (*Romeo and Juliet, Antony and Cleopatra, Hamlet* . . .) or Sylvia Plath's *The Bell Jar,* about an unsuccessful suicide attempt earlier in her life. If a teenager or older family member did commit suicide, it was often hushed up.

Today's teens find suicide in their midst and in their media in much larger measure. It's in the movies they rent—*Heathers, Pump Up the Volume,* and *River's Edge* among them.

It's in the music they listen to—going back to parental hysteria-inducing singles like Metallica's "Fade to Black," Ozzy Osbourne's "Suicide Solution," Storm Troopers of Death's "Kill Yourself," or the Judas Priest album *Stained Class*. (In separate court cases, heavy-metal performer Ozzy Osbourne and members of Judas Priest were vindicated after parents charged that their songs had led to teenage suicides.) Suicide and death remain popular themes in the lyrics of a variety of musical genres today—alternative music in particular.

Millions of American teenagers year in and year out listen to such lyrics and don't kill themselves, say the musicians and their fans, suggesting that parents who blame the music are missing the point. It's not the music that's pushing the kids to do themselves in, some explain—it's their lives, and the misery from which they see no other release.

It Can Happen to Any Teen

Suicide knows no socioeconomic barrier. It happens to honor students with well-to-do parents and all the right friends, troubled teenagers from the worst circumstances, and teenagers in between. It is more common among young people with drug and alcohol abuse problems.

Some of the Whys

"The increase in the teenage suicide rate over the past few decades may reflect the increase in the stressors experienced by adolescents," notes David Elkind, Ph.D., professor of child studies at Tufts University, in his book *Parenting Your Child in the '90's* (Modern Learning Press, 1993). "For example, they have more freedom and opportunity to becomes sexually active and to abuse drugs. They experience more loss (of a parent and of security) due to the drastic increase in the divorce rate. And, on another level, many young people have also lost their belief in progress—the sense that the world is becoming a better place in which to live, work, and raise a family."

A romantic breakup and the seemingly devastating rejection it sometimes entails can also push certain at-risk teenagers over the edge,

Teens Speak on Suicide

"Yeah, we had one girl in our school a few years ago—real smart honors student—blew her brains out," says Kristy,* a gum-chewing 16-year-old girl from a comfortable Houston suburb.

"I had a friend who was suicidal," says Cathy,* a nose-to-the-academic-grindstone 16-year-old from a comfortable Chicago suburb where nearly everybody goes to college. "I think it was partly because she was depressed and having an identity crisis . . . but she's seeing a psychologist now and seems better with it. I've heard of a few others who have done it. I think it's really sad. People shouldn't give up, especially in high school."

The Who and the How

Young women may be more likely to attempt suicide, but young men are far more likely to succeed. Firearms are used in some 60 percent of all youth suicides, according to the U.S. Centers for Disease Control, and males use them as much as seven times as frequently as females. (Young women prefer to attempt suicide with drugs, from which rescue by stomach pumping is possible.) Other popular teenage routes to the ultimate end include slashing, jumping, hanging, and crashing in a car.

according to Loretta Walder, Ph.D., a clinical and school psychologist in New York State.

The Depression Factor

Depression is increasingly common among young children and teens in our country. In its advisory materials for parents, the American Academy of Pediatrics cautions: When depression hits, adults understand that it eventually ends, but an adolescent feeling depressed for the first time may not. What seems trivial to you may devastate teens who are already in a fragile emotional state—so much so that they can't think clearly and see a way out of the problem.

Suicidal adolescents often say they feel isolated and anonymous. Some say attempts to talk about their feelings of unhappiness were ignored or denied by parents pressing them to attain success they themselves never achieved. In some parents' view, depression and complaining are signs of weakness. These parents tell their teens to "buck up" and not show negative emotions.

Suicide Warning Signs

Much has been written on the subject of teen suicide—important reading for parents. Still, many parents of teen suicides say they missed the warning signs that might have saved their children's lives. The American Academy of Child and Adolescent Psychiatry, which provided the following list, advises: Many symptoms of suicidal feelings are similar to those of depression. If your teen displays one or more of these signs of suicidal tendencies, talk to him about it and seek professional help if the depression persists:

- change in eating and sleeping habits
- withdrawal from friends and family and regular activities
- violent actions, rebellious behavior, or running away
- drug and alcohol use
- unusual neglect of personal appearance
- marked personality change
- persistent boredom, difficulty concentrating, or a decline in the quality of schoolwork
- frequent complaints about physical symptoms that are often related to emotions, such as stomachaches, headaches, or fatigue
- loss of interest in pleasurable activities
- lack of tolerance for praise or rewards

Teenagers who are planning to commit suicide may also:

- complain of feeling "rotten inside"
- give verbal hints with statements such as "I won't be a problem for you much longer," "nothing matters," "it's no use," "I won't see you again"
- put their affairs in order—for example, give away favorite possessions, clean their room, and throw away important belongings
- become suddenly cheerful after a period of depression

"Teens are more likely to tell friends than adults when they're seriously considering suicide—and then swear them to secrecy. You, as a friend, have a responsibility to tell an adult. Chances are, you will not lose the friendship. You may well be saving your friend's life."

—Loretta Walder, Ph.D., licensed clinical and school psychologist, New York

According to the American Academy of Pediatrics' experts on adolescent suicide and depression, these themes have been noted among suicidal teens: feelings of hopelessness and worthlessness, the belief that their families don't understand them, a sense that everything is futile, and the belief that they are unable to control their life's direction.

Strategies for Parents and Friends When Talking to a Depressed Teenager

The following suggestions are adapted from the American Academy of Pediatrics' "Guidelines for Parents—Surviving: Coping With Adolescent Depression and Suicide."

1. Listen. Don't dismiss the teen's problems as trivial. To him or her they matter a great deal and are a source of unhappiness.
2. Be honest. If you're worried about the teen, say so. You will not spark thoughts of suicide by asking about it.
3. Share your feelings. Let the teen know he is not alone. Everyone can feel sad or depressed at times.
4. Get help. Find a physician, psychologist, or qualified professional to tackle the potential suicide problem. Don't wait for it to "go away." Although simple depression can disappear as quickly as it came, it can also escalate until an adolescent thinks of suicide as the only way out.

GANGS

When most of the parents of today's teenagers were teens themselves, the closest they ever got to a gang was the musical *West Side Story*.

Today, teenagers come face to face with gangs more often and in more places than most parents want to think about.

"The gangs give poor kids a feeling of recognition," writes Dr. Deborah Prothrow-Stith in her book *Deadly Consequences* (HarperCollins, 1991). "Adolescents want to be noticed. They want to be special, and like all children they prefer negative attention to no attention at all."

The explosion of gang membership and gang violence in the early 1980s saw the problem move from cities with chronic gang trouble—such as Los Angeles and Chicago—to places like Miami, Portland (Oregon), Columbus, Dallas, and Milwaukee, notes a 1993 U.S. Justice Department report. Whereas perhaps ten American cities had gang problems in the early 80s, an estimated 125 report having them now. No community is immune. Today, school administrators in some of the nation's most sedate Midwestern communities find themselves suddenly conversant in the hand signals gang members flash each other as a challenge to fight.

Gang Style: Uncool at School

Teens all over the country, even those at some of the most affluent public and private schools, know all too well about gang symbols, colors, and gestures and the quirks of gang-identifying clothing. Bandannas and caps, for instance, are banned at many schools from coast to coast because of their gang associations. Skinhead violence in the quiet Dal-

Guns and Teen Deaths

Firearm injuries are responsible for more deaths of U.S. teenagers overall than all natural diseases combined, according to the U.S. Centers for Disease Control.

Gun Culture

Guns and fears about guns are a part of the lives of a great many teens today—whether in the city or the suburbs, public schools or private. Consider the findings of a major national study on kids, guns, and violence released by the Harvard School of Public Health in 1993. A cross-section of 2,508 school students in grades 6 through 12 in public, private Catholic, and private non-Catholic schools were surveyed by LH Research, under the direction of Louis Harris and funded by a grant from the Joyce Foundation.

- **Of the 58 percent of suburban students and 63 percent**

las–Fort Worth suburb of Grapevine late last year prompted school officials to briefly ban the wearing of Doc Martens boots because of their storm trooper-like appearance. And the wearing of certain colors, such as the blue of the Crips and the red of the Bloods—the two most widespread and notorious gangs, both of which originated in Los Angeles in the late 1960s—is forbidden in some schools, however innocent it might be.

The trouble sometimes starts because some rap artists wear clothing that mimics gang attire and teenagers mimic *them*.

"To look cool, young people may dress like their favorite rap artists and look like gang members even when they are not, which presents a challenge for schools and parents to determine whether something like an L.A. Raiders jacket is a sign of gang involvement or just the latest fad," notes the recent Gangs 2000 report from the California State Attorney General's Office.

Nasty as They Wanna Be

Kids "walk up to us [in the halls at school] and whisper 'B-world'—for Bloods World—or 'C-World'—for Crips World—and then they walk on," says 14-year-old Brian,* a clean-cut high school freshman in suburban St. Louis County who says he's not sure whether these are really gang members of just wannabes. Despite his hulking build, he admits he's frightened by this behavior.

"Gangs don't have to be in your school to be in your face," says Peter,* a Southern California private school junior who lives in a fashionable area of San Diego. "Gangs make the malls kind of dangerous today," he notes. "When you go, you can't look anybody in the eyes—especially if they're a different race—because if you look them in the eyes, they take it as if you want to fight 'em and they say, 'Hey, you wanna go outside?' At night it gets pretty dangerous because all kinds of gangs from the public schools go there and look for fights. It's pretty scary."

of urban students who said they know where to get a handgun, two out of three said they could get one within a 24-hour period.

- **39 percent of those surveyed know someone personally who has either been killed or injured by gunfire.**
- **4 percent—one in 25—said they have taken a handgun to school in the past year.**
- **11 percent said they were shot at by someone with a gun during the past year.**
- **9 percent said they have shot a gun at someone else.**
- **7 percent reported having metal detectors in their school; 55 percent said they would like to have them.**

In Your Face: Students, Guns, and Violence

City vs. Suburbs	Central city school kids	Suburban school kids
Have been in a physical fight in the last year	19%	20%
Have been suspended for fighting	8%	9%
Could get a handgun if they wanted one	63%	58%
Carried a handgun in the past 30 days	17%	15%
At some time, have been seriously threatened with being shot	15%	12%

Source: "A Survey of Experience, Perceptions, and Apprehensions About Guns Among You People in America," prepared for the Harvard School of Public Health under a grant from the Joyce Foundation. Conducted by L. H. Research; Louis Harris, study director, 1993

Helpful Hints for Bewildered Parents

Demystifying the ins and outs and highs and lows of teenage life is no easy feat. But now that you're a bit more clued in, you may feel ready to take a deep breath and launch into an actual *conversation* with your teen.

Watch Your Way to a Cultural Clue

The following movies are suggested for parental rental if you're seeking insights into teens' sometimes bleak, often funny attitudes toward life:

Slacker
Dazed and Confused
Colors
Boyz N the Hood
Over the Edge
River's Edge
Drugstore Cowboy
New Jack City
Less Than Zero
Say Anything

HOW TO TALK TO A TEENAGER

If anyone knows how to talk to a 90s teenager, it's Barbara Ilardi, Ph.D., professor of psychology at the University of Rochester in New York. One of her specialties is talking with older teens about that hardest of all subjects to discuss: sex. Here are some of her thoughts on how to get teenagers talking on all kinds of subjects.

- To get started: Do the sharing first. It's very risky for a teen when a parent asks, "Tell me what you're thinking." It's much easier if a parent says, "Here's what I've been thinking about this; I wonder what you've been thinking about it." *Don't* start by saying, "So. Tell me how you're feeling about . . . " That's a real conversation killer.
- Talk about yourself. Every parent was a kid once, and often kids have no clue as to who their parents are besides "Mom" and "Dad." Let them know who you are and what life experiences, good and bad, shaped you. Talk about your spouse too. When parents yell at each other—even though some parents like yelling—kids fear they're going to get divorced. They need to know how you feel about each other and things that are happening. For instance, "I really love your mom. I don't know what I'd do without her." Or "I feel like a person all by myself, but I'd be lost without your dad there." If you're divorced, start by talking about your own feelings to help your teen open up.

- Talk about issues. Teens are very interested in and often well informed about current issues: Racism, sexism, the environment, AIDS, and abortion are some of the biggies. Don't be afraid to say how you feel about an issue, but allow your child to feel differently.
- Talk about their college or career interests—and what yours were as a teen. Teenagers need to know you're interested in their hopes and dreams. They also want to hear about how you got where you are, even if it wasn't such a great journey. They need to hear things like "All my life this is what I thought I'd do, but I found out I wasn't any good at it. So I got into this other career," or whatever your experience might have been. Career experiences of other family members and friends can also be of great interest to teens.
- Talk about sex. Kids talk with each other about sex *all* the time and need lots of answers. You really have to be up-front with teens about sex and find a way to firmly anchor your belief system with them beyond just saying, "This is what I want you to do." Try to be realistic and keep an open mind. Share as two individuals with opinions, but don't try to be a friend. Remember, parents are still the ones who set and enforce limits. The relationship is different from friendship, and kids know that.
- Get your teens' views about the future. These are uncertain times for young people. They're hearing that jobs are hard to find, that they'll

Pump Up the Volume
Ferris Bueller's Day Off
Wayne's World
Heathers
Romper Stomper
My Own Private Idaho

Read Your Way to a Cultural Clue

There's lots more information out there for parents looking to unravel the mysteries of teenhood:

13th GEN: Abort, Retry, Ignore, Fail?
by Neil Howe and Bill Strauss
(Vintage Books, 1993)

Generation X
by Douglas Coupland
(St. Martin's Press, 1991)

never be able to equal their parents' lifestyle. Teens are wondering if the degree they get or courses they take today will make any difference. Hear them out about their worries. If you share some of them, your teen may feel less alone. If the fears are unfounded, you can provide reassurance. Perhaps together you can find solutions.

- Talk about family matters. A family illness, a coming vacation, financial pressures—all are subjects teens want to be included in and consulted on. Involving your teen in discussions about important family decisions, troubles, and triumphs builds confidence and communication.
- Finally: Make time to talk with your teen every day. Even if you have only a few minutes to touch base (and that's the case for a lot of parents today), make sure you do. On weekends, find activities to do together—not errands or housework but something you can both enjoy and talk about later. See a movie on a controversial topic. Take a half-day trip to a museum or historic site. Try out a new restaurant together. Attend a sports event. And don't just drop your teen off at the mall. Stop for a snack together on the way there or home, or shop together occasionally for something your teen wants.

HOW TEENS SEE THEMSELVES

The best way to relate to teens is by understanding their point of view and taking their concerns as seriously as they do. Maybe you think you remember what it's like to be a teen, but (especially after reading this book) you should be aware of how much things have changed since you were your kids' age. Here's what some 90s teens have to say about their generation:

"My generation of teens is diverse in its interests and goals. Everyone has a different style and plan for their lives. Our generation is generally very tolerant of other groups, although we don't always understand each other fully. We adapt well to a shrinking world and expanding technologies. I think people don't give teenagers today enough credit."
—Ethan Zweig, 18, North Central High School, Indianapolis, Indiana

"My generation needs major attention. They're not getting it at home. So they experiment with stuff. I think they like to show off or get in trouble. They just need attention, that's all. Parents are at work or they're divorced or they're never at home."
—Justin Unell, 13, Overland Trails Middle School, Overland Park, Kansas

South of Heaven: A Year in the Life of an American High School at the End of the Twentieth Century
by Thomas French
(Doubleday, 1993)

Voices From the Future
by Children's Express, edited by Susan Goodwillie
(Crown Publishers, 1993)

Teenage Wasteland: Suburbia's Dead End Kids
by Donna Gaines
(HarperPerennial/HarperCollins, 1991)

Other good books for parents from medical and psychological experts:

Between Parent and Teenager
by Dr. Haim G. Ginott
(Avon Books, 1971)

You and Your Adolescent: A Parent's Guide for Ages 10-20
by Laurence Steinberg, Ph.D., and Ann Levine
(HarperPerennial/HarperCollins, 1991)

All Grown Up & No Place to Go: Teenagers in Crisis
by David Elkind, Ph.D.
(Addison-Wesley, 1984, 1989)

"My generation is witnessing so many social problems, like gangs and drugs, and no one's really doing anything about them. Adults see the problems, but no one's taking action, so it's going to be an ongoing thing. Also, I think a lot of teenagers today grow up before they have to. They have a lot more responsibility at home. They have to raise brothers and sisters while their parents are at work. They have to look out for themselves. A lot of teens in my generation have dreams too. Very big dreams. I think they'll achieve them if they stick with it. It's not all about being rich; it's also about doing what you want to and being happy."

—Jennifer Carey, 16, Taft High School, Los Angeles

"I think adults, instead of looking at us as future leaders, look down on us as troublemakers who do a lot of wrong. I think a lot of teens are just trying to do the right thing. We're not doing it for the adults. We're doing it to suit our generation. We have our own way of doing things."

—Anjanette Petz, 17, Wilson High School, Wilson, Kansas

"My generation of teens is scary. There are so many teens who are pregnant, already married, quitting school, on drugs, smoking and drinking all the time. My generation, I feel, has no morals, no values. More than half have already ruined themselves at age 15."

—Jancy Berthelot, 16, East Ascension High School, Gonzalez, Louisiana

"My generation of teenagers gets a bad rap. People can't overlook their preconceived notions to see the potential kids today have in terms of everything—sports, arts, academics. People tend to focus on the bad kids. Maybe a small percentage of kids *are* bad. But along with the bad there's a lot of good we have to offer. It's all the fact that adults can't get past the stereotypes they see in the headlines or on the talk shows—the sensational stuff—to see the talents that each individual has."

—Kristina Babbitt, 15, Packer Collegiate Institute, Brooklyn Heights, New York

"My generation is a very confused one, [with] most of us knowing exactly what we want and not doing anything about it. Also, there are some of us who are scared to 'go for it' because of the demoralizing statements coming from peers or parents. Another problem my generation faces every day is the gangster type. They are a constant annoyance, causing nothing but trouble for society. The fact that the gangs are still out there and nothing is being done about it—nothing apparent, anyway—places fear in all of us, which is wrong."

—Aaron Shin, 18, Amphitheater High School, Tucson

"We are a generation of teenagers who fight for our rights."

—Bisrat Abraham, 16, Garrison Forest School, Owings Mills, Maryland

Parenting Your Teenager in the 90's
by David Elkind, Ph.D.
(Modern Learning Press, 1993)

Caring for Your Adolescent: Ages 12 to 21
(a child-care book from the American Academy of Pediatrics)
Donald E. Greydanus, M.D. (ed.)
(Bantam, 1991)

Getting Your Kids to Say "No" in the '90's When You Said "Yes" in the '60's
by Dr. Victor Strasburger
(Fireside Books, 1993)

Deadly Consequences: How Violence is Destroying our Teenage Population and a Plan to Begin Solving the Problem
by Deborah Prothrow-Stith, M.D.
(HarperCollins, 1991)

Crossing Paths: How Your Child's Adolescence Triggers Your Own Crisis
by Laurence Steinberg, Ph.D., and Wendy Steinberg
(Simon & Schuster, 1994)

Video Kids
by Eugene Provenzo Jr.
(Harvard University Press, 1991)

"Guidelines for Parents—Surviving: Coping With Adolescent Depression and Suicide" (pamphlet)
(American Academy of Pediatrics, 1990)

"My generation is dying younger and younger because of AIDS, drugs, and alcohol. Never in my life have I seen so many teens die from alcohol and reckless driving. I see all of these things very clearly because I'm new to this area [southern Louisiana]. I'm a native of San Antonio, Texas. Before I moved to Louisiana last year, I was picturing a place with hillbillies and cows. Sure, there are some of those here, but there are also all the problems of big cities. If the kids here don't get help, who are *they* going to be able to help in the future?"

—Andrew Lessard, 17, East Ascension High School, Gonzales, Louisiana

"My generation of teens is holding the future in our hands. We have the power to be what we want to be and do what we want to do. There is nothing in the world that can stop us unless we let it. We have so many worries, so many responsibilities, and so much hope. I only pray that we do all we can to make our lives and our world a better place. I hope when we leave this earth our children and grandchildren will have easier lives than we've had and they can truly be proud of us."

—Melissa Vink, 18, Pella Community High School, Pella, Iowa